MINING FOR

ALASKAN

ADVENTURES

VOLUME II

COVER PHOTO: Mining in full swing. Rose operates the dragline, while Stan operates the D-8 dozer. The smaller Case 350 dozer is parked in front of the dragline. This sluicing was done after removing the ore with the underground mining method.

PUBLISHED BY:

MAMMOTH ENTERPRISE, GEMALASKA
1023 8TH Avenue
Fairbanks, AK 99701

LARGE PRINT

ROSE RYBACHEK
MINING FOR ALASKAN ADVENTURES
Volume II

If you enjoyed Volume I, you are sure to enjoy Volume II. Read the continuing saga of life in the early 1960's, as lived by one family, and the hardships and joys they shared living in remote Alaska. Then, continue their adventures as they made their living mining the property, and then follow them as they retired. Life can be complicated, but it is worth living when you are having fun.

Published in the United States of America by Mammoth Enterprises, Gemalaska, 1023 8th Avenue, Fairbanks, Alaska 99701

ISBN-13: 978-0692912263 (Custom Universal)
ISBN-10: 0692912266

The Library of Congress has established a Catalog-in-publications record for this title.

Library of Congress Control Number: 2017909423
Mining for Alaskan Adventures, Fairbanks, AK

This large print edition published in accordance with the standards of the N.A.V.H.

Other books by this Author:
Bumps in the Road, copyright 2015
Mining for Alaskan Adventures Volume I, 2017

DEDICATION

Special thanks go to my daughters, for their contribution to this story. Without their encouragement and help, the story would never have been told. Also, thanks to my many friends and acquaintances that encouraged me to put the story into writing. I also appreciate the photos that were supplied by my brother-in-law, Jens Selvig. I also wish to thank Jens for his assistance in helping me do the line drawings in the book.

And, finally, thanks to my proof-readers. Your help has been invaluable

Never let the odds keep you from doing
what you know in your heart you were meant to do.
-H. Jackson Brown, Jr.

INTRODUCTION

Volume II continues the adventures of two placer miners, and their family, as they struggle with everyday disasters, hilarious events, and daily life in remote Alaska.

Stan and Rose Rybachek moved to Alaska in 1958, complements of the US Air Force. They befriended a couple of sourdoughs that lived in the once-prosperous mining town of Livengood. They decided to become placer miners, and in 1963 moved their three small children to the mining property.

The story of their first fourteen-months living on the mining property was described in Mining for Alaskan Adventures, Volume I. Volume II continues their adventures, as they strive to bring the mining claims into production, and produce a livelihood from the gold. Offsetting their income in the early years with trapping, they enjoy adventures that are unique to Alaska.

Follow them as they continue to experience the hardships, but also the rewards of Mining for Alaskan Adventures.

Line drawing of cabin constructed by famous dog musher,
Leonhard Seppala on the mining property. First used by
the Rybacheks as a guest house, but later turned into a
barn for their horses, chickens and calves.

CHAPTER 1

It was the fall of 1964, and our sluicing was finished for the year. "Time to get back to the berry patch," I said. "I want to get another batch of high-bush cranberries picked, and more ketchup made."

We decided we'd park the Weps in the gravel pit just across from the river crossing, and pick some of the succulent looking berries growing on the small peninsula jutting into the Beaver Pond. It was surrounded on three sides by water, and the berries were very lush and plump.

We gave the kids their buckets, hoping they would take the hint, and both Stan and I gingerly made our way deeper and deeper into the peninsula. We could hear the kids yelling and laughing as they played while we picked.

However, soon their laughter changed to shrieks and terrified screams.

"Come on!" Stan yelled, as he raced past me, headed for the cause of the ruckus. I was right behind him.

As we sprinted out of the stand of trees, we could see that the racket was coming from the cab of the Weps. As we neared it, we saw a swarm of hornets inside the truck with the kids. We jerked the kids out of the truck, and got them far away from the swarm. Suzie was stung the worst, having welts and hornet stingers sticking out of her face and hands. She resembled a sparsely-quilled porcupine, with all the stingers protruding from her body. She was also the worst traumatized.

"What happened?" we asked Danny, when his wailing had slowed down to a few sniffles.

"We were picking berries, and having fun jumping over logs, when suddenly Suzie started screaming, and those things started biting us. Then we all ran to the Weps," he replied. "I don't know where all those things came from, but they sure hurt."

He had several welts raising, too. Sallie seemed to have fared the best, with only three welts that we could see.

"We better get these kids home, and put some baking soda on those welts," I said. "But, look at the Weps. It's full of angry hornets. How do we get them out?"

"With the kids gone, maybe they'll just go back to where they came from," Stan said. He sneaked up to the drivers-side door, and opened it, making sure he made a quick get-away. And, soon the swarm did exit the Weps. After swatting a few stragglers, we loaded the kids into the truck, and headed for the baking soda paste. Apparently, that helped with the stinging, because before long, they were happy and playing once again.

"We better see if we can figure out where those hornets came from," I suggested. "Why don't you take a can of Raid and your flashlight when it gets dark, and go investigate?"

You will notice that I didn't volunteer to go with him! Stan returned about an hour later. He had the berry buckets the kids had dropped, although there were very few berries in them. And, he brought our berry buckets, too, since we'd dropped them in the woods when the screaming started.

"I found quite a few holes, and I think the hornets are planning to move underground for the winter. I think I read somewhere that they do that; they hibernate underground. Anyway, I think when Suzie jumped over that log, she landed smack-dab on top of the hornet's winter home. They felt threatened, so attacked the only way they knew how. We need to stay far away from that place next time we go berry picking."

We did not venture out berry picking for a couple of days, but by that time, the welts had all healed, and the kids had *ALMOST* forgotten about the hornets. I did notice, though, when we went to nearly the same area the next time, that they stayed far away from that log.

CHAPTER 2

Winter was rapidly approaching, and the first snowfall of the season was expected momentarily. Stan returned from checking the mail at Livengood, with rather startling news.

"Tony tells me that we have neighbors," he said. "Apparently, some people from South Carolina, or Florida or somewhere down South, have moved into that old Fred Blixt cabin a couple of miles from here, near the spring. Tony says they have six kids, and one is a tiny baby.

"Tony was laughing, and said that the baby was born after they'd crossed into Canada from the US. They had a pretty tough time trying to get out of Canada, since there was no birth certificate for the baby, and they only had five kids when they crossed into Canada … and apparently, a baby had gone missing at a hospital somewhere near where they had traveled.

"Tony says they are real cheechako's. He says they sent their oldest kid to walk the eight miles into Livengood to get the mail, and he didn't even have a warm coat or boots." (Cheechako was a name given to greenhorns in Alaska.)

"Good grief," I replied. "It might be nice to have neighbors, but soon the road will be closed to Fairbanks. They better stock up on supplies while it's still open. I suppose we ought to go meet them, and see if there is anything we can do to help them get settled."

The next morning, we all got into the Weps, and drove over to the old cabin. The whole family gathered around as we drove into their yard, except for the baby. "Hello," Stan said. "We live a couple of miles down the road. We thought we'd come to see you, and welcome you to the neighborhood."

The man shook Stan's hand, and told us to come in. The cabin was very crowded with beds and boxes. But, we did find a chair to sit on. The baby was very cute, and seemed happy.

It was nice to meet them, and they appeared to be very friendly, but quite naïve about what to expect from the coming winter. We had a nice visit, and the kids were happy to have someone their own age to play with.

CHAPTER 3

The first snowfall of the season had occurred, so we knew that winter (and the upcoming road closure) was not far behind. After our harrowing experience of the year before, when we waited too long to make that trip, we decided we better plan a trip to town. The sooner the better.

This year, when the Montgomery Ward and Sears Roebuck Christmas catalogs had arrived in August, we sent in our order for Christmas presents. They had arrived, and we didn't have to worry about Christmas. But, we did need to stock up on other supplies for the winter, such as eggs. As usual, the kids were very excited to go to town. We set off bright and early the next morning. We had no delays on our trip to town.

We got our shopping done and the gas drums filled with gas for the winter. As usual, the kids begged and pleaded that we make a stop at the Dairy Queen for an ice cream cone. So, we did. That was one demand we were happy to give in to.

Our trip home was uneventful. The dogs were very happy to see us, as usual, and jumped around like puppies. Stan and I toted our purchases into the house, and got them stowed.

"Mom, come quick!" Danny yelled. "Something's wrong with Red Dog. Look at him, he crawled under the dresser, but look at that white stuff around his mouth. I can't see his eyes, and he's jerking. Fix him, Mom."

I looked, and sure enough, there was Red Dog writhing around, foaming at the mouth, with his eyes rolled back in his head. I had no idea what had happened to him. We had given both dogs a treat when we got home, so it probably wasn't something he'd eaten. Troop was fine, although interested in watching Red Dog.

We had no clue how to treat him, so just left him alone. Before long, he stopped writhing and lay panting. He was not interested in his dinner that night, but drank a lot of water. We wondered what had happened to him and whether it would recur.

CHAPTER 4

With Thanksgiving rapidly approaching, I suggested that we invite our new neighbors over for Thanksgiving dinner. They had no way to travel, except an old truck that was broken down. Stan said he'd be glad to pick them up, and then take them back home when they were ready to go. He stopped by their place on his next trip to Livengood, offered to take their oldest son with him to check the mail, and presented our invitation. They accepted both invitations.

It was about minus 20°F degrees on Thanksgiving morning, but the Weps started, and Stan was off to get our guests. The kids were very excited, looking forward to company. When they heard the Weps drive into the yard, they raced out in the cold without their jackets.

"I'm so glad you could come," I said, as I ushered the lady into the cabin. "Welcome to our humble abode!"

"You really have a delightful place here," she replied. "It must be nice to have so much room." The cabin they were staying in was smaller than ours, and there were so many more of them than us.

"I brought some of my famous cornbread stuffing," she said. "We like cornbread stuffing, and don't really care for the other kind."

I hadn't known that, so had made a goodly amount of dried bread stuffing. But, I put on a happy face, and thanked her. The turkey aroma was enticing, and soon we all sat down to eat. I tried her cornbread stuffing, but it wasn't the kind of stuffing I'm used to, so I didn't much care for it. None of them even tried my stuffing, so I was a bit miffed about that. They did love the turkey, though, and went through the cranberry sauce I'd made like it was going out of style. And, it was. Good thing we had picked lots of cranberries!

She helped me with the dishes, and while we were talking, I told her about Red Dog's fit.

"I bet he has worms," she said. "Down South, that happens a lot, and we always feed our dogs garlic to get rid of the worms. Do you have any garlic? If you don't, I think I have some you could give him. Just put a clove down his throat every day for a week. If that is what his problem is, the worms will all die and he'll get rid of them. Thank you for a delightful dinner, but I think it's time for us to go home. It's been nice, thank you."

Stan got the Weps fired up, and they loaded up. The kids had to ride in the back, except for the baby, which the lady held. My kids were a little disappointed that their company didn't stay longer and play with some of their toys. But, all in all, it was a great Thanksgiving, and we had plenty of stuffing to eat for the next week.

When Stan got home, I told him about the lady's suggestion as to what might be causing Red Dog's fit. I had lots of garlic, so we followed her advice, and would you believe, he never had another fit?

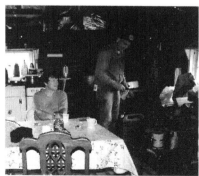

Rose and Stan enjoy a cup of coffee at the cabin

Nice bull moose

Smoker stove, with alder wood – pipe runs to an old
military style wall-locker

CHAPTER 5

Now that winter had arrived, it was time to lay in our winter meat supply. Stan and I went hunting, and I was successful in bagging a moose near the Beaver Pond. Stan butchered it, cut it into relatively small chunks, and hung it in the meat cache to freeze. We could thaw a chunk and it would last us for a week or more. We made our own hamburger, using the hand-cranked meat grinder, and this year, I had found some sausage seasoning spice while shopping in Fairbanks. That, along with a lot of other spices, made a most delicious breakfast sausage.

If we had too big of a hunk of moose thawed for us to eat at one time, we cured it. We had Morton's Sugar Cure, and turned our moose into corned beef. We also cured some for a bacon substitute. We figured it would be best if we could smoke it, so Stan rigged up a smoke house, using an old wall locker that he'd bought at the salvage yard. He used an old camp stove, and ran a stovepipe to the smoke house.

Alder wood made a great smoke for the meat. We were really enjoying our moose.

One day, Stan said, "I wonder how our neighbors are making out? They have all those kids. The road's closed to Fairbanks now, so they can't shop anymore. I think I'll see if I can find them a moose. They could do like we do. I know you overstocked on the Morton's Sugar Cure, and the sausage seasoning, and you could give them some of that, if they wanted."

The next morning, he set off when daylight was just peeking over the hill, with his rifle in hand. It wasn't long before I heard a nearby shot. Soon he was back at the cabin. He had bagged a bull moose, and was waiting for it to cool before taking it to the neighbors.

Moose ready to butcher

"Do you think they have a meat saw? Or knives?" I asked. "They didn't seem to be very well prepared for survival."

"I'll take the meat over to them before it freezes, and I can take along the tools," he replied. "That way, if they don't have the right stuff, I can stay until we have it chunked up, and ready to freeze."

"Want us to come with you?" I asked. "It's been a while since I've visited, and maybe I could help with the meat."

"Sure, why not." He replied. "The more the merrier."

The road was still passable for the Weps, but it was getting harder and harder to get up our hill onto the Elliott Highway. One more trip should be fine, and with the weight of the moose in the Weps, we raced right up the hill with hardly a spin of the wheels.

We drove right up to the cabin our neighbors were staying in. They were very excited to receive the meat. They had never eaten moose meat, but were willing to give it a try.

Stan and the gentleman worked on turning the approximately one-thousand pounds of meat into manageable chunks.

Our kids enjoyed playing with their kids, while I visited with the lady of the house. Occasionally, we'd offer our advice. That's the kind of help I enjoyed giving.

It was starting to get dark before the moose was mostly all hanging from trees in cheese-cloth bags to freeze. We hoped the cheese-cloth would keep the birds away from the meat. She had been happy to get the spices, too, along with instructions as to how to use them. It was time to head back home.

The dogs were happy to see us, and it was good to drive up to the cabin, and see smoke drifting lazily from the stove pipes.

Stan's new Ski-doo gave us many years of service. Here it is pictured in later years with son-in-law Jerry driving, pulling the sled that we used in the 1960s

CHAPTER 6

Stan loved his new snow machine. It was much lighter than the one Curt loaned him. He didn't have to make a trail with snowshoes for this one before he intended going somewhere. Even when the snow got very deep, he could usually ride on top of it. He did have to be careful to watch for overflow when on the river. He was occupied with setting wolf snares, and would soon be setting lynx snares as well.

He had worked hard at getting a large supply of wood stockpiled for the winter. He was still a little lacking in dry wood, and had spotted a few old dead trees downriver that he wanted to add to the woodpile.

One morning he said, "It's fairly warm out, and it isn't far to those trees. I think you and the kids could come with me, and we can get a load of wood. You can ride on that sled I fixed up last summer. I've been using that sled to haul wood with. You can stay by the trees, while I haul the load of wood back to the cabin, and I'll come back to get you."

Never one to miss a chance to do something other than housework, I agreed. We were soon all situated in the sled, with our big old blanket to keep the snow from freezing us. That snow machine kicked up a lot of snow when it was breaking trail, or when the trial hadn't been driven on since the last snow. It was fun being towed along at what seemed like break-neck speed to where the trees were.

While he "said" they were close, they still seemed to be several miles away to me! However, we arrived there safely in a cloud of flying snow. He got out his chainsaw, and sawed down a couple of the large trees. He then used the axe to cut the limbs off, and the kids and I drug the limbs out of the way.

Soon he was cutting blocks off the trees, and we were dragging the smaller ones to the sled, and loading them. It didn't take long, and the sled was loaded, and he was off to unload it. We sat on some stumps, and listened as Red Dog bayed in the distance, apparently chasing a bunny, and using all his lung power. It sounded like he was all around us.

Stan returned for us, and we rode back to the cabin in the sled. It was dinner time, and would soon be dark.

"Where's Red Dog?" I asked. "I haven't seen him since we left the trees. Troop is here, but where's Red Dog?"

"I haven't seen him, either," Stan replied. "I'll go out and call him, maybe he's still chasing that bunny."

Stan grabbed his coat and went out the door. We could hear him calling, but still no Red Dog. We had our dinner, and then it was bed time, and still no Red Dog.

"I wonder if a wolf got him?" I asked. "It seems pretty lonely without him."

When we got up the next morning, there was still no Red Dog. Stan had to check some of his traps, so after breakfast, he left on the snow machine. The kids and I were heartbroken without Red Dog.

When Stan came home, he entered the house carrying Red Dog in his arms.

"I found him in one of my traps way down river from where we were cutting wood," Stan said. "His foot's frozen, and I think it might bleed when it thaws out. So, I think we better bandage it."

We wrapped up the frozen foot in some clean rags, and put him in his bed. Red Dog drank a lot of water, but would not eat anything. His foot did bleed a little when it thawed out, but then it quit bleeding, and we could leave the bandage off. We had no idea what might happen to his foot. He soon regained his appetite. Several days passed, and then we noticed that his foot was starting to shrivel and turn black, and in a week or so, the foot fell off, leaving him with a stump.

We thought that his hunting days would be over, but within a month, he was out patrolling the area once again and chasing rabbits. He may have slowed down a wee bit with only three legs, but he was still able to catch the rabbits. And, we were so pleased to have Red Dog happy once again.

Rose with first wolf pelt of the season

CHAPTER 7

We finished getting the rest of those dead trees hauled home, and the wood pile was looking much better than it had the year before. Winter was settling in, and I was once again running my trap line. I caught a few rabbits, which we either ate, cooked for the dogs, or Stan used as bait. Our routine was about the same as the winter before.

Stan had traps and snares set out in various directions, so he kept himself busy, checking first one direction then the other. And, he usually went into Livengood to check the mail every Friday. Most of the time, he picked up the mail for our neighbors to save their oldest boy from walking that long road into Livengood.

He came home from checking his trap-line one morning, and was very excited.

"Look what I have," he exclaimed. "I finally outsmarted a wolf, and it's a beauty."

He had a beautiful grey wolf on the sled. It had to thaw before he could skin it. We noticed that it didn't have the fleas or lice that the lynx had, so we didn't need to spray it before skinning.

While he was working on the wolf, the kids went outside to play. We were just putting the wolf into its spot to cure, when the door burst open, and Suzie rushed in.

"Mom, come quick," she hollered. "Danny is stuck to the snow machine!"

We raced out, and Danny was bent over the snow machine, looking like he was studying it up close, but hollering at the top of his lungs.

"Grab some warm water," Stan said. "His tongue is frozen to the machine. I froze my tongue on the screen door when I was a kid back in North Dakota, and it hurts like everything!"

We had a bucket of water on the wood stove that was just lukewarm, so I grabbed that, and the dipper, and Stan trickled the warm water over Danny's face. Soon he was free, and, once he could talk again, vowing never to do that again.

He lost a little skin off his tongue, but soon it was completely healed.

CHAPTER 8

In early December, the temperature surprised us by warming up almost to the thawing point.

"I want to go upriver, and scout where I think I saw some beaver caches earlier. I want to be ready when beaver season starts," Stan said one morning after breakfast. "Since it's so warm, do you and the kids want to come with me? We could use that sled we haul wood in, like we did last time, and it would be a nice break for you all."

Again, we never turned down an opportunity to get out of the house, so I agreed. Instead of washing the dishes like I usually did after breakfast, I stacked them for later, got the winter clothes on the kids and myself. The kids and I got comfy in the sled. We had our nice big quilt along, and some water in a jar, just in case someone got thirsty. We were off.

It was almost pleasant on the river, although it had snowed another three inches or so since Stan had last been on that trail. The snow machine kicked up snow that flew into our faces, so it wasn't as pleasant as it might have been. But, it was so very sparking white and beautiful, and, with the fresh snow hanging on the trees, it looked just like a picture post card. We had been traveling about half an hour, when Stan stopped to look at what he believed to be a beaver cache.

"I'll have to check that one out further," he said. "Get back in the sled, I have one more place I want to check."
We were slowly crossing the river when suddenly, water started spurting out around the tracks of the snow machine. The snow machine started slowing down, since it was pulling the heavy sled. Stan gave it full throttle, and it slowly picked up speed. In the meantime, the sled was wallowing around on slush.

Apparently, the warm weather had started a spring to flowing, and with the new snow on top of it, that water hadn't been visible.

Stan finally got the snow machine onto the bank of the river, but the sled was still floating in the water, and slowly sinking, with all of us on board.

Suzie let out a loud cry, screaming, "I'm too young to die!" And, I couldn't have agreed with her more.

I jumped out of the sled, probably not as graceful as a gazelle, but as quickly as I could. I waded to shore, getting wet to my knees, and then helped Stan pull the sled up on the bank. We were all safe, even if we were a bit wet. Fortunately, the sled had remained floating, even with its heavy load, and the kids were mostly dry.

Stan did some probing to locate a safe place for us to get back across the river. He found where the spring was emptying into the river, and above that the ice was solid. In the meantime, my teeth started chattering, and I was thinking about frostbite.

"Time to get back in the sled." I said. "We have to get home before our wet clothes freeze solid."

"I want to walk home," Suzie said. "I really am too young to die."

It took some time to convince her, but she finally believed us, and got into the sled … and we wrapped up tightly in our big blanket. Away we went. The trip home wasn't nearly as picturesque as the one going, but we made it in one piece.

Another tragedy averted.

Danny, Sallie and Suzie. Danny holds Lady, Red Dog's mother

Christmas was much more exciting with presents under the tree

CHAPTER 9

Once again, the kids had their "calendar" ready for Christmas, and were marking off the days as they passed. This year, we were not so concerned about Christmas, since we already had the kids' presents. I had bought Stan several gifts, ranging from more shells for his gun to a new pair of gloves. Where were my presents? I was feeling a little down.

Danny's birthday was December 14, so we decided we'd celebrate it before we put up the Christmas tree.

"What kind of cake do you want?" I asked him the day before his birthday. I was hoping that he didn't want the polka-dot kind, since I had forgotten to buy more sprinkles!

"I'd like chocolate, with chocolate icing. That's my favorite," he replied. "And can we have chocolate ice cream, too?"

"I'm sure Dad can figure out how to make ice cream for us, and I will make you the best chocolate cake you've ever tasted."

Danny helped stir the cake, we baked it, and put the chocolate icing on it. From the outside, it looked a lot like Suzie's cake had, but I knew the inside was very different. Stan packed in some ice, and we made the ice cream.

As usual, Danny was awake way before anyone else on his birthday. He and I huddled in the kitchen, whispering until the girls woke up. Then he got to open one present. He opened the other presents after breakfast. He was thrilled to receive a new truck. Now all three of the kids had new dump trucks. We sometimes let them play with their trucks in the house, but it was dangerous with dump trucks zooming all around our limited floor space. It was much better for them to take the trucks outside and haul snow.

He was disappointed, though, not to get a .22 rifle for a present. He had enjoyed hunting with his Dad using his BB gun, but now that he was six-years-old, he thought he was big enough for a .22. However, his Mom and Dad had different ideas.

The day sped by, and soon it was time for dinner. I made him his favorite meal, meat loaf and scalloped potatoes. All in all, it had been a successful birthday.

CHAPTER 10

The day after Danny's birthday, as we were drinking our morning coffee, Stan said, "I think we should get our Christmas tree cut, and put up today, what do you think?"

"I think we need to wait until the weather is warmer, and the kids and I can go with you," I replied. "Remember that scraggly tree you brought home last year? You were so proud of your 'blue spruce,' but it really didn't look much like a Christmas tree."

"Oh, okay," he said. "We'll wait. But you must admit that tree was pretty nice once I got the extra branches added to it."

I could not argue with that. He had turned a sow's ear into a silk purse, so to speak.

The next day the thermometer started to climb. The kids were excited to think they might get to go on an outing. When Stan returned from checking his trap line, he said, "Get your duds on, we're going Christmas tree hunting."

He already had the sled hooked to the snow machine, but had to unload his "trapping" supplies, and get our big quilt. Soon we were zooming along, checking for trees as we whizzed past them.

When we stopped at a particularly thick patch of trees, I said, "The only trees I've seen that really look like Christmas trees, are the tops of some of those tall trees. How come the shorter ones look so scrawny?"

"Good question. I don't know. Well, we could cut down one of those tall ones, and take the top for a Christmas tree, and then use the rest for firewood." he said.

Grabbing his chainsaw, he did exactly that. Soon we had the most beautiful Christmas tree we could imagine.

"I'll take you guys home, and then come back for the tree," he said. "I probably should chunk up the rest of the tree while its warm, too, and haul the wood home."

We arrived back at the cabin, and after a cup of hot coffee, Stan left to retrieve the tree. The kids and I rearranged our furniture and cleared a place for it. Our cabin was crowded with all our winter supplies, and this tree was much larger than the one we had the year before. Besides, it wasn't flat on one side like the one last year.

Stan returned before dark with a load of firewood, and our tree perched on top. It smelled so good in the cabin, and the very next day, we dug out our decorations.

We had a few decorations that we had used last year, but this tree was larger than last year's tree. More decorations were needed. The kids were a year older, so were excited to think about making decorations. We popped popcorn, and strung it on some fishing line. On some of the strands, we added a few cranberries to make it extra festive. The kids were creative with their colored paper chains, even drawing pictures of who knows what on some of the chains.

Working on the decorations kept the kids occupied for hours, and soon they were putting the decorations on the tree. I cut another large star out of some yellow construction paper, since the one I'd made the year before was badly bent and refused to cooperate. We got that attached to the top of the tree. It looked magnificent.

When the kids were abed, I got their presents wrapped and under the tree. They were excited when they woke up, and found the gifts.

"How come the dogs won't get into the presents this year, like you said they would last year?" Suzie asked.

"The dogs are smarter this year," I replied. I didn't want to admit to her that I had given her a phony excuse for not putting the presents out earlier the year before. I didn't want to admit, even to myself, how close we came to not *having* presents last year.

The next day when Stan was gone, I got out the wrapping paper, and the kids helped me wrap his presents.

Every so often, as Christmas approached, I would check under the tree to see if there was anything for me, but was always disappointed. I finally decided I would have a lot of fun watching the kids as they opened their presents, and it didn't matter if I had a gift or not. (The martyr, eh?)

Christmas morning dawned early. Since the kids were so excited about Santa coming, they were up way before the sun. They were excited to find that he had filled their stockings with candies and goodies that were real treats to them, since they seldom got those kinds of treats. They were happy, and did not want to take a break from playing with their gifts just to have breakfast. However, Mean Mama made them stop, and we had breakfast. Then it was time to open the presents under the tree.

The kids enjoyed opening their gifts. Danny was selected to deliver the gifts, but he had a bit of help from Suzie and Sallie. I had to read him the names as to where each present belonged. He was in a hurry to get his job done, so he could start to open his stack of gifts. Finally, the gifts were all gone from under the tree, and wrapping paper lay strewn all over the floor. I suggested we should have some hot chocolate, before we started clean-up. The kids were not interested in either, chocolate or clean-up!

"Wait a minute," Stan said. "I have something here I forgot to put under the tree." He brought out a gaily wrapped present, and gave it to Danny to deliver it to me!

I was so thrilled that he had remembered a gift for me. The thought crossed my mind that maybe I should just keep the present wrapped, in case he forgot next year, but all four of them were looking at me expectantly. So, I opened the present. Inside it was a beautifully tanned mink hide.

"I couldn't afford to give you a mink coat," Stan said. "But, this is a first installment."

I was thrilled with my mink, and would never part with it. It will hang on my wall until my dying day. I never did get the rest of the mink coat, but who needs one?

My Mink

CHAPTER 11

With the arrival of the New Year of 1965, it was time for Stan to get his beaver traps set. He had finally been successful in snaring wolves, and we now had eight wolf pelts drying, plus he had over thirty lynx hides. It was a good year for trapping.

Almost every morning, depending on the weather, he would load the sled with his trapping equipment. This included: a chainsaw for removing ice for beaver trapping; an ice chipper and scoop shovel for removing the ice residue; snares; traps; and of course, his trusty .22 single-shot rifle. He also carried along lynx and beaver carcasses to use as bait. He had a full sled.

"I think I'll set a few traps in the Beaver Pond this morning before I go downriver to check my lynx traps," he said one morning after breakfast. "I set a really juicy looking trap for lynx downriver, and I ought to have one."

Off he went, and the kids and I did the usual. Chores always included: taking out the ashes (unless I could convince Stan to do it before he left; I was successful about half the time); bringing in wood;

chopping ice to melt for drinking water; and filling the tubs on the stove with clean snow for washing dishes, etc. The kids helped in whatever way they could. Of course, the biggest help was when they played on the chalk board, but I didn't want to tell them that.

Today was baking day. The stove we had was huge, but I was beginning to get the hang of baking bread in it without burning one side of the loaf, and having the other side raw. I decided to bake a very large batch of bread that day. Since the temperatures were below freezing all the time now, I could store it in the garage on the bench, and not have to bake again for a long time.

I tripled the batch I usually made. I ended up with thirteen loaves of bread, two pans of cinnamon rolls and two pans of buns. Stan loved my cinnamon rolls, and I was in trouble if I ever baked without making some. I spent most of the day getting the bread baked, cooled and wrapped for storage.

It was nearly dark when we heard the roar of the snow machine. Stan burst through the door, and exclaimed, "Come see what I have! And, wait until I tell you the story."

We all raced outside to see what he was so excited about and there strapped to the sled, was a wolverine. Now, I've always heard how ferocious wolverines are, and I had never seen one, except in pictures. I didn't even know they lived in this part of Alaska. It was a beautiful animal, although it really had some very long claws and wicked looking teeth.

After we got the wolverine in the house, along with the chainsaw and anything else that shouldn't freeze, Stan began his story.

"I put a couple of holes in the Beaver Pond and set some snares and some traps. There was water in the Beaver Pond this year. I don't know what happened to seal it off, but the beavers should be happy.

"Then, I went downriver, and, remember that set I told you about? The one that was so juicy? Well, the trap was missing. I had it attached to a very heavy drag, too. But, it was completely gone. I could see where it had been drug down river. So, I followed. After what must have been a mile or more, I rounded a bend in the river, and there was that wolverine. The drag had gotten hooked on a twig sticking out of the river ice, and he was fighting to keep going. He must have heard me coming, because he turned and saw me. Instead of trying to get away, he made a mad dash towards me!

"His drag unhooked from the twig, and he headed for me as fast as he could run. It's amazing how quickly a large animal can run when he's mad! I grabbed the .22 and tried to get a bullet in the chamber, but the safety was frozen on safe. I couldn't move the bolt. I jumped up that bank and ran through a stand of willows, as if the devil himself were chasing me. He almost was!

"Just as I hoped, the wolverine got the drag hung up in the willows, and had to stop. You never heard such a racket as he was making, growling and howling; yanking on that drag and still trying to get me; and I think he was frothing at the mouth. He was one mad wolverine.

"I took off my gloves, and used my warm hand to thaw the safety loose, and then I shot him. It took me three bullets before I felt safe enough to go near him.

After I finally decided he was quite dead, I circled around, and went back to get the snow machine. He hadn't moved when I got back, so I figured it was safe to load him up. This is the first wolverine I've ever caught, and isn't he pretty?"

Stan got him skinned, and modified the stretchers to accommodate his pelt. It was such a beautiful pelt that we had it tanned, and decided not to sell it. We had it for many years, until our house in North Pole was robbed in the fall of 1986, and the pelt was stolen. Now all we have are memories of that ferocious beast.

Wolverine, photo by Joel Sartore, National Geographic

Stan's brother Ralph
with Wolverine hide

Stan's favorite lynx
notice white foot.

Ralph with a selection of furs caught by Stan

CHAPTER 12

Spring was upon us and everything was beginning to melt. Stan pulled his traps before breakup. He ended the season by catching ten wolves, much better than the year before. He had learned. He also had about fifty beavers, plus nearly forty lynx, and a few mink, martin and muskrat. It was going to be a big payday when the fur buyer showed up in Fairbanks.

"I think we'd better get the pipeline put back together," Stan said one morning. "It's about time to get the water in the ditch moving again. Hopefully we can get more gravel to sluice this year." Yes, it was Mother's Day again. Although Stan didn't mention that.

Our sluicing had been pretty limited the year before, since we hadn't been able to uncover much gravel. However, we had several ounces of gold to show for our work, including that first nugget we'd found in the sluice box.

Off we went, leaving the kids at home, with promises that they would not get into anything, but would play on the chalk board. I brought out the colored chalk, which was a treat for them, and hoped that would keep them occupied.

An hour or so later, we got the pipeline put back together. On our way home, I asked. "Do you know what day this is? It's Mother's Day again. Why do you always pick Mother's Day to put the pipeline together? What do you have against Mother's Day?"

"Oh, I forgot," he said, and grabbing a pussy willow, he handed it to me, and said, "Happy Mother's Day."

I couldn't stay angry with him after that, could I? The kids were still happily playing with their colored chalk when we got home. They were looking forward to being able to play outside once again, and planning on how they were going to mine some gold this year.

Pussy Willows in bloom

CHAPTER 13

The days were getting longer and the nights shorter, as we edged towards the end of May. We noticed that the dogs were on edge, and would often bark or growl for no apparent reason. And, we noticed that some things in the yard seemed to move.

We bought a new barbeque in Fairbanks the last time we were in town, and had just tried it out once. It somehow got upset in the yard. Some other unimportant things were moved, such as the rain barrel. Plus, our dump looked like it had been disturbed.

"What do you suppose has the dogs so nervous?" I asked one morning. "Any chance a bear is hanging around? They probably haven't been out of hibernation long, and maybe we have one that's looking for a handout?"

"It could be," Stan replied. "I've seen some fresh sign of bears along the ditch. In fact, I've started packing my .357 again, just in case Red Dog gets any fancy ideas of teasing a bear again. Having lost his foot doesn't seem to have slowed him down much. He's still as feisty as ever."

We went to bed that night and I had trouble sleeping, thinking of what might be lurking in the dark. It was just getting daylight when I thought I heard something in the garage. We left the outside man-door open all the time when it was above freezing. I inched out of bed, and peered out the window. I couldn't see anything out of the ordinary in the garage. Then, I slowly scanned nearer to the window, and there right under the window, peering back at me, was a huge black bear.

The dogs were still peacefully sleeping, thank goodness. And so was Stan. I gently shook him awake, and whispered about the bear being in the garage.

Stan stealthily got out of bed and went to where he had his Winchester 30.06. He inched his way to the door, and slowly opened it. By that time the dogs were awake and growling slightly. They apparently had no idea what was happening, though, because they were not making a whole lot of noise.

However, it was enough of a commotion to send the bear scurrying out the door with Stan (in his underwear) hot on its heels. The bear raced around the cabin and across an opening towards the back cabin. Stan finally got a clear shot at it, and the bear fell in a heap. Stan came back in the house, but when he opened the door, both Troop and Red Dog bolted out the door.

We went to the kitchen window to watch what the dogs would do. Red Dog had his nose to the ground, and was baying for all he was worth, hot on the trail of the bear. Troop stopped at the side of the cabin and offered his support, long distance.

Poor Red Dog didn't recognize the bear, and stumbled right over it. He got to his feet, looked at the bear, barked a few times, and jumped backwards. He did that over and over, barking and then jumping backwards, until he and Troop were both at the edge of the cabin, giving that dead bear what for. Stan and I were laughing so hard, we had tears in our eyes.

Later, Stan went out and skinned the bear, and I made sausage out of it. The sausage was tasty, although we had a mental problem, thinking about eating bear meat.

We did eat some of it, but mostly gave it away. Our new neighbors loved it. We were not bothered by nosy bears after that.

CHAPTER 14

One morning the kids were getting ready to go outside to play. Suzie and Sallie wanted to play Cowboys and Indian, but Danny was adamant. "That's a kid's game," he said. "I want to get my BB gun and go hunting!"

The battle was raging when I suddenly had an idea. "How would you like to go fishing today?" I asked. The river was low, and it should be a wonderful day for fishing. Stan had cut some fishing poles from willows and rigged them with flies. He and I would often sneak down to the bridge, and dabble our hooks in the water, but we had never taken the kids.

The kids began jumping up and down, and screaming, "Can we, Mom?" I had opened a door that would be hard to close!

"Yes, right after we get our chores done," I said. Before long, they were racing around, dust was flying, and the dogs were hiding, afraid they were going to get trampled. All thoughts of playing Cowboys and Indian, or going hunting, had fled.

"Get your boots on," I said. "And, remember, you need to sit perfectly still on the bridge, and don't jump around. *IF* you catch a fish, raise your pole slowly, and drop the fish into this five-gallon bucket that I'm taking with us. Can you remember that?" I asked.

"Oh, sure," Danny replied. "Don't worry about us, we just want to catch breakfast!"

We walked to the river. Well, I walked to the river, but the kids raced ahead of me. I had to yell at them to stop before they ran out on the bridge. I carefully sat them on the edge of the bridge, spaced out so that the danger of them catching each other was minimum. We could see a fish or two swimming around in a pool under the bridge, and there were a couple lounging along the bank in the sun on the far side of the river.

We got the poles lined out, and the kids began dabbling their flies in the water. It wasn't long before Sallie let out a whoop. "I've got one," she yelled. She had a nice grayling on her pole.

"Bring it carefully up on the bridge, and put in in the bucket," I said.

As she was raising it, Danny yelled, "I have one, too."

"Wait until I get Sallie's in the bucket, and then lower yours in." I instructed. As I was moving towards Sallie's dangling fish, it squirmed off her hook and flopped back in the water.

"Don't worry," I told her. "You'll catch another one soon." I gingerly eased my way over to where Danny's fish was dangling, and before I quite had the bucket under it, it also wiggled off the hook and splashed back into the river.

All this time Sue had been quietly watching with her big brown eyes. She then timidly said, "Mom, I have a fish, too."

She had raised a fish out of the water, and it was trying hard to get off the hook.

"Bring it over this way," I told her. She gingerly brought the fish over, and it landed neatly in the bucket.

She was ready to go home then. "I have my fish for breakfast," she said. "I'm tired of fishing!"

"Well, you can go sit on the bank and watch," I told her. "But, you need to let Danny and Sallie have a chance to catch another one. You can't be the only one eating fish."

She obediently got up from her seat on the edge of the bridge and made her way to the bank. There she sat, contentedly watching as first Danny, and then Sallie landed a fish in the bucket.

"We can't quit yet," I said. "You need to catch a fish for your Dad, and what about me? I need one, too!"

It wasn't long before two more fish were in the bucket. We took them proudly home, Stan cleaned them when he got home, and we all enjoyed our fish breakfast.

From that day on, Danny was torn between going hunting or fishing. Usually fishing won.

Willow fishing poles, one leaned against the meat cache.
Notice fly near bottom of pole on right

CHAPTER 15

Mining season was in full swing again, and Stan was very busy with the ditch. He often asked me to take care of the pond, and run the giant when the pond was full. The kids were older and tired of making mud babies. But, they did enjoy exploring.

I was washing the mine face one day when I spotted something that looked unusual at the bottom of the permafrost, and just above the gravel. We had found a lot of wood, in various stages of decomposition, that had washed off the mine face. I had even found some green leaves on one of the twigs, but by the time I had gotten it to the house, it had turned black. We were told that if we found any bones, they would be between 15,000 and 30,000 years old, so we figured that the wood was probably that old, too.

Anyway, I finally shut off the water and went to investigate what that strange looking stuff was. There was a deposit about six inches in diameter, composed of tiny pellets, and who knew how far back into the hill it might go? It looked like little

BB's, and was substantially different from anything we'd seen before. I managed to scrape some off, and put it in a handy gold pan. I took it to the cabin when the kids and I were finished for the day, and stashed it in a plastic bag. The kids and I prepared supper, and had it ready for the table when Stan got home.

As he came through the door, I grabbed my bag of material and showed it to him, asking, "What do you think this could be? It looks like there's a large deposit, but I couldn't get any more, since it's still frozen."

He looked at it thoughtfully. "I think it's poop of some kind. But, I have no idea what kind. Too big to be mouse and too small to be rabbit."

I could glean a little bit more every time before we ran the giant, and soon had nearly a pint of it. The next time we went to town, I took some of it with me, and made a stop at the University Museum. The lady at the front desk was as mystified as I was, but said she'd have their people look at it, and perhaps do an analysis and let me know. The deposit in the ice ended and there was no more of whatever it was.

I was happy when a month or so later, I received a letter from the Museum. They said that it *was* manure from a Coney or a Pica, a member of the rabbit family. Apparently, some still live on Cleary Summit, between Fairbanks and Circle.

They thanked me for the sample I had provided them and said they would be happy to accept any further items that we washed out of the hillside. I wished I had been able to preserve those green leaves, but they were history.

The next bit of excitement came when I noticed a strange looking rock with a hole in the center. It was lying on the gravel after I'd washed the face. There was a layer of vegetation and sticks that were about fifteen-feet above the gravel. I had no idea if my rock had fallen from the layer of vegetation, or been on the gravel to start with. I thought it resembled one of those things that the Indians used to grind corn and other seeds. Was it a mortar? It looked like it had been flattened on two sides, but the hole in the center was perfectly rounded.

I picked it up and was excited to show it to Stan when he came home.

"Do you think that could possibly be a human artifact?" I asked. "Look at how it has such a perfect hole in the center."

"Looks to me like one of those things the Indians used to grind corn with," he replied.

"That's exactly what it looked like to me, I said. I'll take it to the museum the next time I go."

A few days later the kids and I were back on the road to Fairbanks. After doing the shopping, we swung by the University. The lady at the desk took one look at my rock and said. "I think that's where a round rock was dislodged from the bigger rock. I'm sure it has nothing to do with early humans in Alaska, and we're not interested in it."

I was disappointed, but did not toss the rock away on her say-so. I even found a long, narrow stone that could have been used to pound the corn. I never did get a second-opinion, but always wished I had. (See photo page 60.)

CHAPTER 16

It hadn't rained for a long time, and the water was low. Stan was almost exclusively washing the ice face which gave me a break. Occasionally, he would ask me to "wash the face" but the times were rare.

He returned from washing the face one day in a jolly mood. "You'll never guess what I saw thawing out of the ice," he said, "you'll have to come and look at it now, before the mud thaws more and covers it. I don't know what will happen the next time I wash the face. And, since it's almost your birthday, you can have it!"

I've had that superstition about something good always happening around my birthday for years. This was great!

Never one to pass up an invitation, I got the boots on the kids, and we hiked up to the mine area. There, in that layer of vegetation fifteen feet above the gravel, in the middle of what appeared to have once been a grassy meadow, was a leg protruding. It looked to be the leg of a sheep or goat, but the interesting thing was that it was still covered in hide. Oh, it was shrunken and blackened with age, but it was very different from anything I'd ever seen before.

"What do you think it is?" I asked.

"I have no idea, but do you see that hide on it?" he said. "This's really interesting. We're getting a bird's eye view of what the area looked like thousands of years-ago. I heard that people found remains of large beavers that were six to seven feet tall, and weighed around two-hundred pounds. I guess they lived somewhere between twelve-thousand to two-million years-ago. See where those sticks are piled up on our layer of vegetation? That could have been a dam in the creek, and this grassy looking area could have been a lake behind the dam ... and that critter may have fallen in and drowned."

We kept watching the leg-bone, and soon discovered that it was attached to a large chunk of hide. I couldn't believe my eyes one morning, when I saw Troop go up to the face, and drag a hunk of the hide out of the mud. He sprinted away with it in his mouth and ignored my demands that he put it down. He sat atop a pile of tailings and chewed on the old hide. If I tried to take it from him, he ran, but didn't drop the hide.

Every morning after that, when Stan would go to wash the face, I would race up ahead of him and try to beat Troop to whatever may have fallen during the night. He was probably the only dog in the world that chewed on hide thousands of years old.

My parents came shortly after my birthday, and Mom baked me a belated birthday cake. Stan got ice, and we had ice cream. But, the best present of all was the critter melting out of the ice.

By the end of June, I had gathered the skull, complete with the dried brain rattling around inside. I had found the esophagus and all four of the legs. I also had large chunks of hide that I beat Troop to, along with miscellaneous bones. I carefully washed and dried them and put them high up on a shelf, out of Troop's reach. We eventually gave most of my critter to the University Museum, but I kept the leg.

Artifact or rock?

Mastodon jawbone, tusks and teeth from our mine

CHAPTER 17

Stan kept busy improving our cabin. He'd purchased a five-hundred-gallon water tank, mounted it on a trailer, and parked it on the hill beside the cabin. When the tank was nearly empty, he would back the Weps up to it, hook on to it, and take it to the river to refill. The water in the river was not nearly as colored as the water in Wilbur Creek.

I had to make a run into Fairbanks for some parts to hook up the tank, and while I was there, I decided to look for a propane-fired hot water heater. That would make him a very thoughtful birthday present, one that we could all enjoy. I found one and bought it. I also did the grocery shopping and noticed that they were selling fireworks. July 4 was not that far off, so I stocked up on fireworks, too. I knew that Stan enjoyed setting them off, and we would enjoy the show.

"Wow," he said, when he saw the fireworks. "I have never had fireworks for a birthday present. And, I'm so glad you thought of the water heater. I was thinking that should be our next purchase."

He installed it that very day in the bathroom. This meant we had hot water whenever we wanted it, available in the bathtub.

He never did get around to plumbing the kitchen sink, but it was so much handier to just go to the bathroom to get dishwater, than it had been to haul it from the creek and heat it. And, it was heavenly to sink into that large tub of hot water. The kids loved it, believe it or not. They had their toys, and often would get to splurge and use some bubble bath.

No longer did we have to use the small, round laundry tub for bathing. That had been a hassle, since we'd start with the youngest, then the next, then the next, and finally it was my turn. We added hot water as we went along, but usually had to bail some out, since the longer the bathing night went on, the larger the person in the tub, and the fuller it got. Finally, Stan got to bathe in our dirty water, but he didn't seem to mind and never complained.

My parents and siblings really enjoyed the bathtub, too. Especially my Mom, who liked to soak in the tub before going to bed every night.

With all the company, the water tank emptied rather quickly. One morning Stan said, "I have to get water today. Want to help me hook up the trailer?"

After breakfast, he got the Weps and backed it slowly up the hill to hook to the trailer. I walked up the hill to the trailer and started giving him hand signals; go left, go right, come on back, etc. (Hand signals were not my strong point, and sometimes we would nearly come to blows, since what I was trying to tell him wasn't always what he was receiving! I thought he paid no attention to my signals, and he thought my signals made no sense.)

On this morning, we were doing quite well and were getting close to being able to hook the trailer up. However, we soon discovered that a family of wasps had built their nest under the fender of the trailer. When I accidently bumped the fender, they came roaring out with vengeance on their minds (if they have minds).

They were attacking me right and left, and I panicked. All I could do was jump up and down, swatting my arms, face, and anywhere else they were stinging, while screaming at the top of my lungs. I was carrying on this losing battle when I felt strong arms reach out and yank me out of the way … it was Stan. He had come to my rescue. We made a hasty retreat to the cabin where I dug out the baking soda and made a paste. I had many welts of varying sizes, depending on when I'd smacked the stinging wasp. Stan only had twelve. He was my hero!

When it got dark, Stan took the Raid out and eliminated the wasp nest. The next day, we completed hooking the water tank to the Weps, hauled it to the river, filled it, and then he backed it into its parking spot. I helped direct him on parking, all the while crunching on the dead bodies of annihilated wasps. I didn't even feel sorry for them, not even a little bit.

The company that visited us the next day said we looked like alien life forms straight out of Star Wars with all our welts.

CHAPTER 18

A few days later, Stan came back from washing the face and was excited.

"You need to come and see what's washing out of the face now," he said. "I couldn't believe it."

"Well, what is it?" I asked. "Tell me."

"No, you have to see this to believe it," he replied. We all walked up to the mine. There, protruding from our layer of vegetation over the gravel, was another leg-bone. But, this was not from a small animal. It was huge. It must have been over a foot in diameter at the joint and looked like it was about four feet long.

"What do you think that's from?" I asked. "Could it be a wooly mammoth or a mastodon?"

Leg bone after it was removed to our basement in North Pole. Holding it is our good friend Garnet

"It just about has to be one or the other," Stan replied. "I don't know how you tell the difference but it sure is big. I hope it doesn't break when it falls. I'm going to leave some mud under it, so it should have a soft landing. I'd like to see Troop try to make off with that one!"

My parents were fascinated with the huge bone, too. They had no clue as to what it might be, either.

A few days later we were running low on flour, and with Mom visiting (who loved to bake), this could not be.

"I need to go to town and get flour and a few other groceries." I said. "Anyone want to go with me?"

My kids were having too much fun playing in the creek. With the low water, they could make dams and play in the mud to their heart's content. My sister Betty wanted to stay home and "take care of the kids." (I always figured she had her nose in an enjoyable book.) Dad also volunteered to stay home and so did my brother Henry and sister Debbie. It was just Mom and me that made the trip.

I gathered up the skull from *my* critter and hoped that we'd have time to take it by the University to see if they knew what animal it might have come from. While I was about it, I took some other miscellaneous bones, such as a skull that I thought might belong to a skunk.

We had a perfectly nice trip to town. We got a whole pickup load of things we just couldn't live without, and, we even remembered the flour.

I had spotted a jar of pickled hearing in the grocery store and bought it for Stan. It would be a nice belated birthday present. He loved pickled herring, and he bought himself some every chance he got. He never had to worry about me raiding his cache. It didn't even smell good to me, and he didn't have to share it with the kids either, since they had the same opinion of it that I had.

We did have time to go by the University, and I talked to the lady there about getting an identification on my collection of bones. I told her, "I have this box of bones that we've washed out of the face on our mining claims, and I wonder if you folks could identify them? I'll be back to town in a couple of weeks or so, and I can stop in and pick them up. And, I have another question. We have this big old bone that's slowly emerging from the face, and it looks like there are several other large bones in that area. How do you tell a mastodon from a wooly mammoth?"

"I have no idea," the lady replied. "But, I'll ask our people, and maybe when you come to pick up your box, I'll have an answer for you."

Mom and I left the box and headed back up the Elliott highway. We thought we'd be home in time for a belated lunch, so we hadn't bought anything for a snack. At home, we had home-made bread and leftover meat from a moose roast. The moose cached in the old mine shaft was coming in mighty handy.

As we rounded a bend in the Elliott Highway, we came upon an accident. An oversized truck had turned over right in the middle of the road, and the road was blocked. The driver came to our pickup and told us that someone had gone back to Fairbanks to see about getting a large wrecker to come and open the road, but it would be several hours before we could get through.

For some reason, just knowing that we were without lunch made us very hungry. Flour, sugar and Crisco are not palatable. We had nothing edible except …. we did have Stan's pickled herring. After thinking about it for a while, we decided we could choke down just one piece, and maybe that would satisfy us.

I cautiously opened the jar, and we each had a piece. It slid down quite well. Then, one piece led to another, and before long, we had devoured the whole jar. It was delicious. To this day, when I think of pickled herring, my mouth starts to water. Strange how your viewpoint on things change in the blink of an eye.

It was nearly dark when the wrecker finally arrived and got the truck upright and out of the road. We went on to the cabin, but I was careful to hide the empty pickled herring jar. Stan never did know how close he came to enjoy his delicious present.

What he could have had!

Stan and Rose with Wooly Mammoth Tusk

Collection of bones including the Wooly Mammoth
jawbone

CHAPTER 19

We could hardly wait until our next trip to town to see if the Museum had been able to identify any of the bones we had taken them. So, I was elated when Stan came home one morning a couple of weeks later and announced, "I have to go to town. I need to get some more tie wire. I thought I had another roll, but I've looked all over the place, and I can't find it. Some of the pipeline is falling apart, and I really need the wire." (Of course, he located the wire a day after we returned from town with his tie wire, but we had the excuse we wanted.)

I immediately volunteered to go to town for him, and Mom was more than happy to go along. We set off together in the Weps once again. We were lucky to find his wire at the first place we stopped. Of course, no trip to town would be complete without a swing by the grocery store. We did that, making sure we had snacks this time … and finally, we stopped by the Museum to see if they had identified our bones.

"Yes," the lady said. "We've identified everything. The one with the hide is a Musk Ox. The little skull you brought in is a baby wolf. We don't have a baby wolf skull, and would love to have it for our display. We wrapped it up carefully to give back to you. If you ever want to donate that, we would be more than happy to receive it."

She continued, "One of those antlers is from a prehistoric elk, and that odd shaped one is from one of those giant beavers. You have quite a collection there, but whatever happened to the large bone you were telling me about?"

"Well, it thawed loose, and we have it in a safe place," I replied. We've recovered a bunch of other large bones from nearby, too. We have quite a few rib bones and a lower jawbone. We also found some tusks, which we think are curved like a Wooly Mammoth. It has really been exciting seeing what will thaw out next."

"We're interested in anything you care to donate," she said. "Please keep us in mind." She did not tell us how to tell the difference between wooly mammoth and mastodon.

We gathered up our box of bones, and the little skull, which I had thought was probably from a skunk, was neatly wrapped in cotton in a small box.

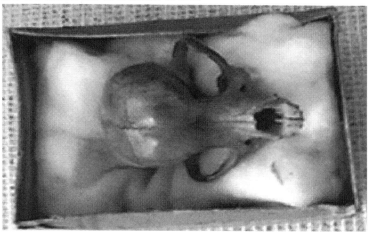
Baby wolf skull in cotton wrapping

I still am not sure they correctly identified the critter that had the hide on it. The skull looked more like a sheep to me, but what do I know? Anyway, we had an identification, and were happy.

About a week later we heard the unmistakable sound of a helicopter coming in for a landing near the mine area. Stan was washing the face at the time. All was quiet for a while. Since I'm rather nosy, I had about decided I should go investigate, when it lifted off and headed back towards Fairbanks. It wasn't long before Stan came home, with a large grin spreading across his face.

"I don't know what you told those folks at the museum," he said, "but, they just hired a helicopter and came out here, hoping we'd donate our intact mastodon. Somehow, they got the impression the hide was from a mastodon that was all in one piece, and they wanted to get it back to Fairbanks before it thawed!"

I was aghast at how that rumor had spread. It was not even close to what we'd said. It *was* possible to find something like that since it had been only about fifteen years since the story had been told about a group in Russia that served 250,000-year-old Wooly Mammoth at a grand ball-room dinner. Unfortunately, we didn't have anything quite as exotic.

Mound of bones

CHAPTER 20

Every time the kids and I got a chance to go into Livengood for the mail, we went. One day when I was talking to Tony, I happened to mention that I would like to make some root beer, and, if I got real adventuresome, some real beer.

"Would you like some beer bottles?" Tony asked. "I have a lot of them just sitting around out back. I hate to throw them away, but I don't have much use for empties."

That sounded like a great idea, so we hauled fifteen-cases of bottles home and stored them in an old boiler. I ordered some bottle caps, and a corker. Once they arrived, I set about making several batches of root beer. The kids sure loved the root beer.

Then I got very ambitious and decided to try my hand at making real beer. Mom had been helpful making the root beer, so I asked her if she'd help me make real beer. She turned me down!

I made it myself, and was very careful to test it with the hydrometer as it aged. When I thought it was time to bottle, we got out a siphon, and emptied the large crock. Since it was summer, and we were not using the wood stove in the kitchen, we stored the bottles of beer in their cardboard boxes behind the stove to age.

My parents had lived in the Fairbanks/North Pole area for about five years before they moved back to Montana and had made many friends. One-day Mom asked if some of her friends from church could come to visit. I, of course, said sure, they would be welcome. I told her to just let me know when they were coming, and we'd fix a nice lunch.

Arrangements were made, and they arrived one morning. The men all went up to look at the mining operation, and to just visit, while the ladies gathered around the kitchen table. One lady, the wife of a pastor, was quite intolerant in her views.

Soon, the conversation turned to beer. "I would not have a bottle of beer in my house," she said. Little did she know that I had at least five cases stacked right behind her. "I think beer is the devil's own brew, and I wish that it was outlawed."

I had to reply to that. "I think if a person drinks beer wisely, it isn't bad. I agree that over indulging is not good, but having a beer occasionally can't hurt. Besides, Jesus himself turned water into wine, so he must not have had anything against alcoholic beverages, in moderation."

"Don't you believe that," she said. "That's just a figure of speech, and Jesus would never drink alcohol of any kind."

I didn't want to argue with her; after all, she was Mom's friend. But, it did sort of open my eyes as to why Mom had not been willing to help me make the beer. I knew that Mom never took a drink of alcohol and now I knew why!

The men returned, and we all had a nice lunch. And, soon the company left, headed on their way back to town.

The very next morning as I was sweeping the floor in the living room, I heard a large explosion coming from the direction of the kitchen. I raced out to see what had happened, and discovered, to my chagrin, that one of the bottles of beer had exploded. Maybe I had bottled it too early? I was afraid to try to move my cache of beer or clean up the mess that the exploding bottle had made, because I was afraid some others might be volatile, too.

We just put up with the stench of green beer, and, believe it or not, the aroma wafting from it smelled rather enticing, once you got used to it.

It wasn't long before another bottle and then another blew up. If it had been the Fourth of July, we would have been celebrating in style! Fortunately, the broken glass was all confined to the cardboard cases, but they soon began dripping. Before the next couple of days were over, nearly half of my beer had exploded.

The rest of the bottles must have been tougher. But, the beer was still explosive. When we opened a bottle, we had to open it over a dishpan, since the beer would come out frothing. It didn't taste bad once it settled down, so Stan, my Dad and I enjoyed our homebrew. I was very careful to read the hydrometer correctly the next time I made beer. After all, I only had twelve cases of empty bottles left!

CHAPTER 21

It was the 4ᵗʰ of July. We planned a huge cook-out, and Mom and I made potato salad, deviled eggs, and baked beans for our picnic. We had invited Marty, Garnet, and their daughter Roxanne up for the occasion. They arrived right on time. The moose burger was all ready to put on the grill. And, our mouths were watering.

"Are you ready to cook?" I asked Stan. "The burgers are ready for you, and I think everyone is starved."

"We can't have dinner until after we set off some of those fireworks you got me," he replied. "I'll get just a few and then, once we have a mini-celebration, I'll get the grill going."

He grabbed a bag of fireworks, and the matches and headed out the door with Marty right on his heels. Before long, we heard a string of fireworks. Since our work was finished, the rest of us trailed them outside to see what they were doing. Not satisfied to just make a lot of noise, they soon rounded up some cans and had a contest to see who could blow the can the highest into the air.

It was nearly an hour later that Stan got the grill lit. Finally, we had lunch. The burgers were delicious, and we all enjoyed a wonderful 4th of July.

Marty sets a firecracker, while Elizabeth, Henry, Garnet, Roxanne, Stan and Dad look on

Elizabeth watches fireworks (left) while Henry appears frightened. Garnet and Roxanne, with Sallie on hood

CHAPTR 22

Stan came home with the mail one sunny August day and was very excited.

"Look what I have," he exclaimed. "I finally heard from the Civil Service people on Eielson Air Force Base, and I have a job. I need to report to work the first week in September."

Earlier, we had a long talk and discussed the possibility of home schooling Danny, who would be entering first grade that fall. We talked about what an experience it was for the kids living at the mine, but the kids were missing out on interacting with other kids. We decided we should put them in school.

Danny would be starting first grade. Suzie would go to kindergarten, and Sallie would stay home with me until the following year, when she would enter kindergarten.

"I guess we could go to town tomorrow and take care of the paperwork. I can find out just when I need to report for work, plus I need another big bolt before I can put the sluice box back together. You remember when I moved it last fall, it sort of came apart. We can't have that," he said.

So, off to town we went. My parents opted to stay at the cabin. We knew that if we were going to enroll the kids in school they needed to be current in their inoculations, so the kids got to go with us. We stopped by the clinic, once we reached town, and were told to come back later that afternoon. They told us how much each shot would cost. We did not share this information with the kids.

We had a nice visit with our renters, but they were sad, knowing they would have to move. However, on the bright side, we should be able to play pinochle all winter long, depending on what kind of shift-work Stan might have. I stayed to visit with our friends, while Stan made the trip to Eielson. He soon returned with a big grin on his face. He would be working straight days and not shift-work. We could have a normal life!

It was soon time to go by the clinic and get the shots. Again, we did not confide our destination to the kids. They had been sad up to that point, since they had not been able to buy anything. When we reached the clinic, I gave them each a couple of dollars and sent them on their way. They were so excited. Finally, they were about to get to buy something! They raced in waving their money. I guess I shouldn't be surprised that they felt betrayed (and rightly so) when they found out they were at the clinic, and the only thing they could buy was a shot or two. I, of course, followed them in and once they had received what they'd paid for, I tried to console them.

They were beyond consolation, so the only thing to do was stop by the DQ again. That seemed to pacify them.

We arrived back at the cabin, loaded with groceries and Stan's bolt. The next day he began working on the sluice box. It didn't take him long to have it ready to go. I was happy to have Mom and Dad there to keep an eye on the kids, while Stan and I sluiced long hours.

One morning as Stan was pushing gravel to the sluice box with the dozer, he stopped, got off, and stood staring at the ground. Then he got down on his knees, and was really doing an inspection. I was hoping for a gigantic gold nugget, but he soon got back on the dozer and delivered the gravel to the sluice box. Unfortunately, his hands were empty.

"What did you find?" I asked, when he finally came near enough for me to question him.

"Well, I saw a hole open up in the gravel behind the dozer. I think it's an old mine shaft. It looked to be about four-feet deep, and while I couldn't see very much, it looks like a tunnel heading off in that direction," he said as he pointed toward the upper cabin.

We continued sluicing, but he stayed far away from the hole with the dozer. When we shut down for lunch, we both walked over to have a look. Since he had seen it early that morning, it had grown; it was a rather large hole now.

Without thinking, Stan jumped down into the hole. He ducked down to see what he could see and then started gasping and choking. Thoughts raced through my mind. What could I do to help? Was he just going to die in that hole? He finally straightened up, and with his head sticking out of the hole, he began taking deep breaths. What a relief that was.

When he could finally talk, he croaked out, "There isn't any air down here. It's been sealed up so long there is no oxygen. It really grabbed my breath, and I nearly blacked out. I need to get out of here. If you get the crowbar and lay it across the hole, I think I can get out."

I ran off for the crowbar and put it across the hole, and he swung himself out. Several days later, he again jumped into the hole. The oxygen had made its way into the hole by that time, and he had no trouble breathing. I leaned in as far as I felt safe, peering into the tunnel. It was very interesting to see a pair of old overalls cast aside on the floor and a gold pan leaning up against the gravel wall. We did not trust the roof of the tunnel, so he (fortunately) did not venture far from the hole. And, I just looked.

Soon thereafter, we finished sluicing, and we had more gold dust and nuggets to add to our collection.

Gold pan with penny to show size

Clean up process. Stan and Mom work the gravels loose in the riffles, and then use the smaller clean-up box to sluice. They use a wash tub to catch the concentrates, then finish the operation using a gold pan. The gold scales weigh the cleanup.

CHAPTER 23

It was nearly Sue's birthday, and I wondered what kind of birthday cake she would want this year. On other birthdays, she had wanted orange, and then green polka-dots. What would this year bring?

So, I asked her one morning as we were getting ready for a trip to town. "What kind of cake do you want for your birthday this year?"

"I want a chocolate cake, with chocolate icing, and chocolate ice cream," she replied.

I was quite surprised at her request. "How come you don't want something odd like you had before?" I asked.

"I just want chocolate," she replied. "That's what Danny had, and that's what I want."

This was easy and didn't take any special ingredients. I could use the old standby Betty Crocker Cookbook. And, with my Mom there who loved to bake, it should be an exceptional cake. It was. The ice cream was delicious, and the day was perfect. She enjoyed her "girl" presents, and was soon busy combing Barbie's hair.

A couple of days later I asked Sallie what kind of cake she wanted, expecting that she would want the same as Suzie. She surprised me, though.

"I want a blue cake, with green frosting," she said.

"Are you sure?" I asked, as I went for the food coloring. "You want this color of a cake, and this color for the frosting?"

"Yes, that's what I want," she replied.

Betty Crocker saw us through another yellow cake, and we added the blue coloring. It slightly resembled a blue sky and was not too revolting. That is, until we put the green frosting on it. The cake then resembled a misshapen bale of hay.

"So, what about your ice cream?" I asked. "What kind do you want?"

"I think I'd like white ice cream this time," Sallie replied. "I really like that kind best, and I think it will look pretty with my cake."

I wasn't sure anything could make the cake look pretty, but if that was what she wanted, that was what she would get.

Stan brought down the bag of ice, and we had lots of help turning the crank since my siblings were there. I told them that if they helped crank, they would get to help lick the paddle. They were arguing the whole time over whose turn it was to crank.

Sallie was very happy when she opened her gifts. She had several "girl things," but her favorite was once again a truck. This was not a very large truck, like her dump truck, but a smaller one that she could haul in the larger dump truck. Back to play on the hill they went, and built a few more roads.

The hill was an ideal place for building roads, and it resembled some of the modern-day freeways.

Toys like the ones the kids loved to play with

CHAPTER 24

"I guess we'll help you move back to town," Mom said one morning. "Then we'll hit the road back to Montana. We need to get settled in for the winter, too, and get the kids back in school." So, we had a plan.

In the meantime, I was no longer having to race Troop to see which one of us would be the first to find hide from the musk ox. It had all fallen to the ground. However, the other animal, the wooly mammoth or mastodon, still had a few bones that were thawing out. We had already accumulated a huge mound of bones, and more just kept coming. We coated them with Tung-oil in an attempt to preserve them, and once that had soaked in, we stock-piled them in the machine shed.

"What do you think we should do with all those bones?" I asked Stan one day.

"I guess we need to just leave them here in the machine shed, and cover them up with a tarp," he said. "We don't have any place to store them, and hopefully no one will steal them. They are pretty impressive."

"I am amazed at that lower jawbone," I said. "Did you notice those two little ivory tusks sticking out of it? You can pull them out, and put them back in again. And, look at those teeth. You can tell that the animal was a grass eater, since the teeth are flat. I think it's a mastodon jawbone."

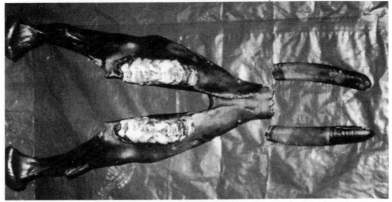

Mastodon jawbone

"I did notice that," Stan said. "And, did you notice that other jawbone, with those two little square front teeth? He had one big tooth and one little tooth on each side of his mouth. I think that's a wooly mammoth jawbone."

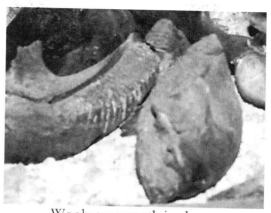
Wooly mammoth jawbone

We covered the bones securely with a tarp, and they were still there the next spring when we came back. We were very happy to see them.

NOTE: The saga of the bones is almost like a mystery thriller. We built our house in North Pole in 1975 and had a four-foot crawl space under the whole house. We moved our bone collection to the crawl space. I joked that we had a skeleton in our basement, and we almost certainly did. Then, between 1988 and 1993, we were involved in several automobile accidents and could no longer work at the mine. We sold the bones to a guy that told us he was in contact with an Asian market, and they were interested in buying bones.

He reconstructed the animal and determined that it was a mastodon; a rare sub-species that had not been found in Alaska before. We apparently had parts of two animals, which he thought were twins, since they were the same size. One animal was over 90% complete, while the other was about 45% complete. Before he had completed the sale, the bottom dropped out of the Yen, and his deal fell through.

Our buyer with the completed backbone of Mastodon #1

Part of the skeleton of Mastodon #2

He stored the bones in a storage container in Anchorage. A few months later he unexpectedly died. Of course, that meant he quit paying rent on the storage unit, so the owners opened it a few months later. They were shocked to find this huge stack of gigantic bones. They called the police thinking someone had committed murder, of what kind of critter I have no idea!

Fortunately, one of the professors at the University of Alaska knew the history of the bones, and that they were legally in private ownership. The man's brother inherited them. In 2016, he donated them to the University of Alaska, where hopefully they will end up on display in the museum one day.

Bones and Tusks found by the Rybacheks

Miscellaneous bones from mastodon and wooly mammoth

Collection of tusks found by the Rybacheks

CHAPTER 25

My parents and siblings decided to leave earlier than they planned, since they discovered that school in Montana also started around the first of September. So, they were off.

Ready to go: Debbie, Henry, Betty, Dad and Mom ready for the trip to Montana

We moved back to your house in North Pole in early September and soon had the kids enrolled in school. They had their first week of school under their belts. Stan was ready to start work on Monday. We decided we should make one last weekend trip to the mine, just to make sure the cabins were ready for winter. Bright and early Saturday morning, we were once again on the Elliott Highway.

We "winterized" the cabins by putting supports under the roof in both cabins. This should keep the roofs from collapsing; we didn't want to find them on the floor next spring. By evening, we decided everything was buttoned up as well as we could make it, and it was ready for winter.

When we'd driven past the Beaver Pond coming in, we'd spotted a few ducks. Most of the ducks and other water fowl had already left Alaska for their winter habitat, but, surprisingly, a few were still there.

"I think I'll go duck hunting early tomorrow morning. Want to come with me?" Stan asked. "We can go before the kids wake up, and even if they do wake up, they'll be fine for a while."

Never one to turn down an invitation, I was waiting for him when he was ready. Troop came along; there was no leaving him at home after he'd seen Stan pick up the shotgun. He could hardly contain himself, and watered every tree.

As we neared the Beaver Pond, Stan whispered, "Be sure and stay a bit behind. Troop will sneak up with me, but if I shoot, he'll be off like a flash. He'll leap in the water. I don't want you getting between him and the water, or you might be joining him."

I followed ten paces behind, and was again fascinated as Stan crouched down to be shorter than the willows, and Troop crawled along on his belly. I saw Stan put the gun to his shoulder, and then "Bang!" he fired. As predicted, Troop was off like an arrow, and leapt into the pond with a mighty splash. The rest of the ducks flew off with a loud noise.

"Hey, I shot a goose!" Stan exclaimed. "I had no idea a goose would still be anywhere around this time of year, but there he is. Come on and watch Troop get him."

So, I edged up to the side of the Beaver Pond. I watched in awe as Troop, with powerful strokes, neared the downed goose. Imagine my surprise, as well as Stan's, when Troop swam right around the goose and came back to shore. He gave Stan the most disgusted look, and then sat down behind him, as if to say, "Dummy, you missed the duck!"

"I don't think he's ever retrieved a goose before," Stan said. "He didn't recognize it. I'll send him back out, and hopefully he'll figure out what he's after this time. I'd hate to have to get the boat out again this fall, just to get the goose, but it would no doubt be worth it. That goose will surely taste good!"

Off Troop went on Stan's signal. As before, he just swam around the goose and headed back to shore. This time the look he gave Stan was even more disgusted than the first one had been.

"One more try," Stan said, "and then we'll have to get the boat."

Off Troop obediently went, and this time, as he was swimming past the goose, a slight breeze came up. It ruffled a tuft of feathers on the goose. Without hesitation, Troop swam to the goose, grabbed it, and hauled it to shore.

"Good boy," Stan said. "You deserve a treat for that. You saved us from having to drag the boat all the way from the cabin to the Beaver Pond, and then back to the cabin!"

As predicted, the goose was delicious.

CHAPTER 26

Our kids had been fairly isolated from civilization for three of their formative years. Thus, when we moved back to our house in North Pole, they were fascinated with some of the things that most people take for granted.

One day I watched in amazement as they each stood by an electric light switch. First Danny would turn his on, and they would all "ooh" and "aah." Then it was Suzie's turn, followed by Sallie. They had the lights blinking off and on like a lighthouse. They were amused for several days with the light switches, until it grew boring. I didn't want to spoil their fun, so let them play.

I will never forget the first day that I gave the kids a shower in our walk-in shower. Again, they were amazed.

Suzie said, "Mom look, the water comes out of that strainer, and we don't even have to dump it!" She was right. The shower head did look like a strainer, although I had never thought of that before.

The kids were also fascinated with the television, and it took almost an act of God to get them to go to bed at night. With school in progress, they needed to be in bed by eight. Sometimes that was a challenge. After we put them to bed, Stan and I would usually watch a program. It wasn't unusual to look around and see three heads peering around the corner of the living room.

One day, we let them finish watching Gunsmoke, and then shut off the TV. We were going visiting. Across the street from our house lived some good friends. They had a daughter that was just a year older than Danny, and a son that was three years older. I thought the kids would be very happy to go visiting their friends.

We knocked on the door, and were told to come in. Which we did. They had their television on, and were watching the Ed Sullivan show, which came on right after Gunsmoke.

We sat down to talk, but in a few minutes, we noticed that our kids were huddled in a corner. They were not paying a bit of attention to their friends.

Finally, Danny approached, and said, "Mom, can we go home? We have cowboys on our television." They did love those cowboys. Of course, the programs had changed, and we no longer had cowboys on our tv, either. We had to take them home to show them that we really didn't have cowboys at home!

Our friends had just gotten their amateur radio operator licenses. We were quite interested in talking with them about ham radio. It was very expensive making phone calls to the Lower 48 states. They talked about making phone patches. Apparently, you could talk to a ham somewhere in the states, and he could run a phone patch. You would only have to pay long distance charges from where he was to where the person was you wanted to call. This really sounded great to me, since my parents were back in Montana, and I only talked to them once a year, with the high cost of long distance phone calls.

After we'd satisfied the kids they were not missing cowboys at our house, we returned. They were content to sit and watch The Ed Sullivan show, while we picked the brains of our friends.

Going home when it was nearly bedtime for the kids, I said to Stan, "Do you think we could do that? You would have no problem taking the theory test, since you work on teletype machines, but I'm not sure I could pass it. We also have to do thirteen words per minute of Morse code. What do you think?"

"Well, if John and Eloise can do it, and Marty and Garnet, I don't see why we can't," he said. Yes, Marty and Garnet had also gotten their licenses.

We ordered some study manuals, and in the spring of 1966, an examiner came to Fairbanks from Anchorage. Examiners only came two times a year, so it was our opportunity to get our license.

We both passed the theory, but when it came to the code, we both failed. Stan was in trouble because he tried to print, and he just couldn't print that fast. I was in trouble because I was so nervous that my fingers were like ice.

"Can I try again?" I asked the examiner.

"Do you think it would make any difference?" he replied, very condescendingly.

So, I reached out and touched him with my ice-cold hand. He jumped, but then he agreed that I could try once more.

I sat in a corner with my hands wrapped in my coat, and finally they felt comfortable. That time, I passed the test. I was happy. Stan received a Technician license, with the call of KL7FQR and I received my General, with the call of KL7FQQ.

Stan passed his General in the fall, after practicing his cursive writing. The next year, we strung up a wire antenna at the mine, and from then on, we had communications when one or the other of us was there on our own.

Note: Ham radio has been a big part of my life since that unforgettable day in 1965 when I first heard of it. I was very active on the radio, and made some exciting contacts with famous people. Probably the most notable was with Jordon's King Hussein and Queen Alia, JY1 and JY2. I also made a contact with Senator Barry Goldwater, who was an outspoken Senator.

During the Fairbanks flood in August 1967, all communication with Fairbanks was lost. The telephone terminal was in a basement, and covered with water. The only communication that was available was ham radio. The authorities set up a communications center at the University of Alaska. Since it was located on high ground, it was dry.

We were living at 12-mile on the Richardson highway near North Pole, and were fortunate that our house was built on a man-made hill. We were surrounded by water, but our house was high and dry. Stan and his buddy Val worked to get the Weps located near the house, and got our radio on the air using battery power from the Weps.

I spent over twenty straight hours passing messages between a station in Washington, and the University. There were a couple of interesting things that happened, besides the satisfaction of letting loved ones know that their family was safe.

We got an emergency call from an engineer in Washington that had been involved with building the Post Office. His message was that they should not pump out the basement when the water receded. He said the building would collapse. I was able to relay them message just in time.

The person I talked to said they were just dragging the pumps over to start pumping.

I often received updates as to what was going on with the flood, and I relayed them to my friend in Washington. One day, my aunt who lived in Coeur d'Alene, Idaho, heard a familiar voice coming over the radio. She listened, and it was me, giving one of the updates. They had recorded it, and played it over the radio.

Fairbanks was without electricity for about ten days, and during that time I passed many health and welfare messages. I was honored when the Department of Health, Education, and Welfare, Region IX awarded me a citation in recognition of my contribution to the flood communications. This was the first time that a non-employee had been awarded this particular citation.

One other bit of ham radio history dealt with the U.S. Coast Guard Cutter Glacier, that was in the Antarctica for Operation Deepfreeze during the winter of 1967-68. They operated under the callsign of KC4USG, and I often ran phone patches for them.

One day, they wanted to run a phone patch to Point Barrow. They had a young man in their crew whose family lived there. I was quite surprised when I got the family on the phone, and they began talking in their native language, which I believe to be Inupiat. The only words I could understand were "over" when it was time to switch from one speaker to the next.

I was very surprised when a month or so later, I received a picture in the mail. It was a picture of a young man talking on the radio, with a big sign saying, "1000th p/p". Apparently, I was lucky enough to have run the 1000th phone patch that the Glacier had made since it left port.

CHAPTER 27

We would never again be snowed-in at the mine. We did continue to spend as much time as we could there during the summers, and we made a few visits during the winter, but we never again spent a whole winter there.

Sometimes Stan would have a month off during the summer for his vacation, other times he could take the whole summer off as unpaid leave. The kids and I usually spent most of the summers at the mine. Stan and I decided we didn't want to go into debt to buy equipment for the mine, so it took us a long time to get the mine on a paying basis. However, it was a wonderful place to raise the kids.

We liked to get away from town whenever we could, and the cabin was a delightful place to go. We were there one Sunday afternoon in early spring, getting ready to crawl back on the snow machine and go back to Fairbanks, when we heard a knock on the door.

"Come in," Stan hollered.

In walked two men, dressed very warmly and perspiring heavily.

One gentleman said, "did you hear that truck go off the road last night?"

"No," Stan replied. "What truck?"

"Well, one of our trucks went off that big cliff up there on the Elliott, and is down in the flat. We were wondering if you could get your dozer started and pull it out?"

"You mean, a truck actually went over the lookout? Was the driver killed?"

"No, he doesn't seem to have a scratch on him. In fact, he said that if you could pull him out and the truck would start, he'd be happy to drive it back to Fairbanks. Can you?"

"Well, I can't this weekend. I have to go back to work tomorrow, but I could do it next weekend, if that would be okay with you. I need to warm the dozer, and get it fueled, and I just don't have time left today," Stan said.

"That would be fine," the man replied. "We'll be glad to pay you whatever you want."

They left, and we finished packing the food things we needed to take back with us. Soon we were on the road, too. As we got to the lookout, we could see where the truck had gone over the edge.

There were no tracks for a long way, and then there was a trail of debris through the trees and tundra. Apparently, the truck had been airborne for some distance. We were surprised to see it sitting upright at the end of its trail of destruction.

Our arrangements were to meet the guys Sunday morning at 10:00 am. We went to the mine on Friday night, and on Saturday, Stan got the dozer fueled, started and warmed up, and the rollers all thawed and rolling. On Sunday, we drove the dozer to the flat. The guys were a few minutes late but soon showed up.

"How did you manage this?" Stan asked Gil, the driver, when he was introduced to him.

"I must have gone to sleep, because the next thing I knew, the change in sound woke me up. I glanced out the window and I was airborne. I couldn't think of anything to do but get on the floor boards, and hang onto the gear shifts. You should have heard those empty barrels I was hauling when we first hit. We hit and bounced, but kept on going, and it sounded like we were shearing off trees as we went. I don't ever want to do anything like that again."

The snow in the flat was only about two feet deep, but with the uneven tundra, it was rough getting out to the truck. But soon Stan had the log chain on it, and it was headed out. Amazingly, the truck started once it was on the road, and Gil drove it back to Fairbanks.

Gil's truck pulled by the dozer

Some of Gill's friends installed this marker that read "Gill's Landing" where he made his leap. Looking across the Tolovana valley toward the mining claims.

CHAPTER 28

In early August 1967, we were devastated by the loss of Danny in a drowning accident. We were in town, getting ready to spend a month at the mine when the accident happened. We cancelled our trip. About two weeks later, a monumental flood hit the Fairbanks area and we were active on the ham radio. Somehow, helping others helped us to feel like living again. In December of 1968, we welcomed our last child, Cyndi.

Our friend and the owner of our mining claims, John, passed away. His brother Tony inherited all of John's assets. Tony was feeling his oats, and moved a gal at least forty years younger than he was into the Livengood Inn.

A few months later, the two of them traveled to the "Old Country" (Yugoslavia), so she could meet his relatives.

Stan and I were in town shopping one day, a few weeks after they left, when we ran into a friend of ours.

"Have you heard the latest about Tony?" our friend asked.

"No, what is Romeo up to now?" Stan asked.

"Well, the story is that he and Myra made a trip to Switzerland from Yugoslavia. Myra left Tony sleeping in their hotel room. She took all his clothes, money and passport, while she hopped a plane back to Alaska.

"Before Tony and Myra left Fairbanks, Tony put her name on his bank accounts and on his safe deposit box. She could access his assets in case something happened to him. And, she made sure something did happen! They say she cleaned the box out. I know he had quite a lot of money in there. Apparently, she wrote checks on his account, and drained that. She has also been trying to sell all his property, since he gave her a Power-of-Attorney."

"Wow, that's quite a story," Stan said. "So, what happened to Tony? Is he still naked in Switzerland?"

"I guess he had quite a time trying to convince the authorities who he was, and how he'd come to be in that predicament. Apparently, his kinfolks had to send him money for new clothes and fare back to

Yugoslavia. I don't know what he did for ID papers. That's all I *do* know, except that Myra has been running all over town with a guy she claims is her "financial advisor," but apparently he is from the same city in Canada that she is, and they are petty cozy."

Stan and I started talking about Tony's predicament on our way home.

"You know," Stan said. "Tony now owns the claims we've been working on. And, if Myra can sell them, we'd be out on our ear. I think we ought to go to the recorder's office and file a location notice on the claims."

The very next day, we were at the Recorder's office with our location notice in hand. We never heard from Myra, but a couple of years later, Tony came back to Alaska with his nephew. We were at the cabin when they drove up.

"Tony," Stan said, shaking his hand. "I have to tell you that we've jumped your claims. But, we intend to buy them from you. We heard what happened and didn't want Myra to be able to sell them out from under us."

"You are good friends," Tony replied. "This is my nephew, Nick. We brought you some plum wine from the Old Country. My niece makes it, have a glass."

We sampled his "plum wine" and it was very strong. Tears streamed down both our faces after a tiny sip. That was some potent brew! We were not unhappy when he repacked the bottle.

Nick was not interested in listening to our discussion about the claims, so he disappeared outside. Tony agreed that we could buy the claims from him, and we settled on a price. When Nick returned, he had six squirrels that he'd killed by throwing rocks. The kids were wide-eyed thinking what a dead-eye Nick was with rocks. They didn't want to make Nick angry, in case he might pick up a rock!

And, Tony was happy that he at least had some of his possessions preserved from the greedy fingers of Myra.

Sue, Cyndi and Sallie

CHAPTER 29

Stan diverted the creek shortly after the spring thaw one year, so that it was nearer our operation. This also meant the creek was running down a new channel, one that it had never run down before. The first time we had low water in the creek Stan came home very excited.

"Come look," he said. "There's a lot of gold showing up in those rocks just above the water-fall. It sure looks pretty."

The kids and I made our way to the area he had mentioned, and you could see the gold nuggets shining in the sun. They were partially hidden in natural riffles in the new creek bed.

"How can we get them?" I asked. "Even though the water isn't that high, there's still a current, and if we mess with the nuggets, they're sure to sink."

"We better wait until the water drops a bit more." he said. "Then, we should be able to use tweezers to get them. Do you have a good pair of tweezers?"

I did, and we patiently waited for the water to get low enough for our nugget recovery. Finally, it was time to go with our tweezers, and begin plucking out the gold. We lost a few nuggets when they fell off the tweezers, but we had quite a good collection going. We harvested nearly an ounce before the rains came, and the creek rose. But, for several years after that, we would go out with our tweezers, and look for gold every time the creek got low. The kids loved to help with that.

Now that Wilbur Creek was taking a new path, we had to cross the creek to get from the cabin to the mining operation. When the water was high, this presented a problem, so Stan built a small bridge over the creek. He dragged cables across the creek in a narrow spot. He then nailed some planks on cross boards. It ended up being a very scary bridge. It would not have been quite so scary if the cables didn't bounce when you walked on them. Besides, there were no hand rails to hang onto.

The kids and I made many trips across that bridge, but it was an adventure every time we needed to cross it. The kids were quite sure-footed and bounced across it without fear. I took my time and didn't relax until I was on the other side. As far as I know, no one ever fell off the bridge.

Hannibal makes his way across the shaky foot bridge, while Sam stands guard (with his stick) on the far side

Stan and I invested in a pump and installed it near the newly diverted creek. With the pump, we could retire the ditch and pipeline. This would allow us to remove the overburden much quicker, since our source of water was more reliable.

Our Waukesha pump

One thing we noticed was that the face thawed much faster just above the gravel, and we ended up with a large overhang of frozen muck. Most of our frozen muck was water. When it thawed, it just ran off. Eventually, though, mud would build up on the ice, and slow the thaw. It was best if we could wash mud off a couple of times a day.

When Stan was bringing in the gravel for sluicing, he would often run the dozer under the overhang. Being under the overhang with the dozer looked dangerous to me. Occasionally, we would see where a fairly large chunk of ice had fallen off the face and lay thawing on the gravel. But, he thought it was worth it to scrape as much gravel as he could get, and he could get under the overhang ten or twelve feet.

It was still a scary thing to do!

CHAPTER 30

The kids were getting older, and Suzie and Sallie were great helpers. They took care of Cyndi when I was busy at the mine. They also pitched in to help at the mine when there was something they could do. And, they did a lot of chores at the cabin. Often, they had a nice, hot meal ready when we got home.

Suzie and Sallie both loved to fish, and I told them they could go to the river and fish when the water was low, if they watched Cyndi very carefully. Of course, they needed to complete their chores first. They enjoyed that independence a lot.

I returned home one morning, and they had the door to the cabin locked. I pounded on the door, and they finally unlocked it.

"What's going on?" I angrily asked. "You don't have to lock the door when you're home!"

"Mom, we were scared," Sue replied. "We finished the chores and went fishing. We went down near the mouth of Wilbur

Creek, and we caught four nice fish. We had them in the bucket and were thinking of coming home, since one of them was big enough that Cyndi and I could share. But then, we thought we heard something snapping a twig in the trees. We listened closely, and we heard it again."

"We thought it was a bear, Mom." Sallie chimed in. "We talked about grabbing our bucket of fish and running for home but decided that a bear could run faster than we could. Especially since we had Cyndi with us, and she has short legs. So, we took the biggest fish out of the bucket and left it on the ground."

"We ran a little way," Sue continued. "Then, we stopped and left another fish. We ran a little way again and left another fish. And, we ran again. By that time, we were at the bottom of the hill near the cabin and we left our last fish. We made it to the cabin, but decided to lock the door in case the bear wanted more fish!"

"Well," I replied. "I didn't see any bear sign when I came home. I'm glad you're all right, and it's too bad about the fish. Maybe we can get the gun and go back to retrieve the fish. That way, we'll have a delicious breakfast tomorrow."

I got the .357, and told the girls to come. They reluctantly followed me out the door. As we neared the bottom of the hill, I said, "I don't see any fish here. Are you sure you dropped one?"

Both girls answered in the affirmative, and Cyndi nodded her head. I was surprised we found no fish. Where was it? Anyway, we continued down the road.

"I think this is about where we put another one," Sue said. But, again, there was no fish there! Could the girls be right that they were followed home?

By this time, I was beginning to get a bit concerned that perhaps there might be some unfriendly critter waiting in the bushes looking for another handout.

"This is about where we put the next one," Sallie said, and she pointed to a patch of dirt. No fish there, either.

"I'm not sure we need to go the rest of the way," I said. And, we turned tail and went home.

Either the girls were right that a bear was enjoying their fish, or the birds were having a feast. We never found out what happened to our breakfast.

Suzie, Cyndi, Stan and Sallie pose in front of our very picturesque "white house." This started out as a tent house, and then was modified with some lumber

Sue, Cyndi and Stan pose with the old giant. Notice the Black Shack in the background

CHAPTER 31

School was finally out and the girls and I, along with our menagerie of chickens, ducks, geese and rabbits, moved to the mine for the summer. Stan was working that summer, but he would come on weekends, and whenever he could get time off.

It was almost time for my birthday so I expected something special to happen. Stan was to come to the mine on Friday evening, and my birthday was Sunday.

"So," I said on Friday morning to Suzie and Sallie, "are you girls going to make me a birthday cake? We can chip off some ice and make ice cream once your Dad gets here, but what about the cake."

Sue piped up with, "What kind of cake would you like, Mom? Want one with polka-dots?"

"No, nothing that fancy! I'd be happy with a yellow cake with chocolate frosting. We have the makings for maple nut ice cream. We can butcher a chicken and have a real feast," I said.

"Do you think Dad will bring you a present this year?" Sallie asked. "He does remember sometimes. We bought you something when we were in town. We're keeping it a secret, though, and you'll not find out from us what it is."

They were being sneaky, and I was intrigued. I was happy that they were getting old enough to remember birthdays and anniversaries. I continued to wonder, what could they have bought me?

Stan arrived on Friday night as planned and had dinner with us. But, early the next morning, he disappeared without saying where he was going or what he was up to. We did our chores, and I ran the giant, wondering where he was. He usually ran the giant when he was around. The girls got the cake made, and Stan brought the ice for the ice cream, once he showed up again.

The next morning was my birthday, and he disappeared again. This time he wasn't gone long, and showed up with a long package. He stood it in the corner and would not let me open it until we enjoyed the cake and ice cream after dinner.

Imagine my surprise to find a homemade garden hoe. He had shaped the head, mounted it on a pipe, and then attached it to an old handle he'd found. The girls gave me a most gorgeous necklace.

Another delightful birthday.

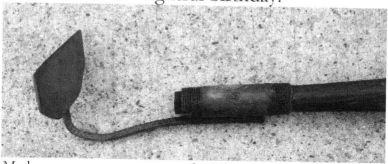

My hoe gave me many years of service. In fact, it is still in use today, over fifty years after it was made

Friday was Stan's birthday, five days after mine. He had the whole next week off from work. The girls and I made him a couple of rhubarb pies, as per his Birthday Tradition. He arrived late that night and was happy to see the pies cooling.

"I need some help moving the giant," I told him. "We need it closer to the face, since I'm wasting a lot of water. I bet we can put a couple more pipes on the pipeline."

"We'll go up first thing in the morning," he replied. "Can't have you wasting water! By the way, how is the water holding out? We've been getting a lot of rain in Fairbanks, but what about here?"

"Not so much," I replied. "I haven't had to wear rain gear all week. I wish it would rain a bit more. As it is, I'm only getting to wash for about forty-five minutes a couple of times a day. Then, no water."

The next morning, we had our coffee and then breakfast and were ready to go.

"You girls get your chores done, and then you can read or do whatever you want. We'll be back in plenty of time to get dinner," I said.

Imagine our surprise when we arrived home that afternoon to find a delicious fried chicken dinner waiting. It really smelled good. Not only was there fried chicken, but they had made mashed potatoes and broccoli. We sat down to the table and were looking forward to that delicious meal. It was quite a shock when we tried to stick a fork in the chicken. It was very tough!

"Where'd you get the chicken?" I asked the girls

"Oh, Mom," Suzie replied, "We decided we'd surprise you with a fried chicken dinner for Dad's birthday, so we went out to find the right chicken. We thought that if we got one that had mostly lost her feathers, it would be easier to pluck. So, we selected one that was really molting.

"I was a bit afraid to try to chop her head off, but Sallie wasn't. I held the chicken, and Sallie whacked. The first time she missed entirely. Then, the second time, she got part of the neck cut. It was horrible. Blood was spurting everywhere, and the chicken was squawking and flopping around. She got loose and started running around. We finally caught her, and then Sallie whacked again. That time, she got the head off except that it was hanging on the neck by just some skin. I turned the chicken loose, and she chased us. It was horrible."

"Well," Sallie chimed in, "I would have done better if I hadn't closed my eyes every time I swung the axe. I tried to keep them open, but they just closed, and I never knew where the axe was going to land. But the worst part came when we tried to pluck her, and where she had no feathers, she had lots and lots of pin feathers. It was the worst chicken I've ever tried to pluck."

I was quite upset, too, to learn that they had butchered my best egg layer. But, their heart was in the right place, just their knowledge was a bit lacking.

Notice the hen on the left that has lost most of her feathers? She was probably having a last meal ...

Marigolds grow profusely in an old mining bucket used in the 1930's when John and the mining company mined using a shaft

CHAPTER 32

On a nice, warm day in July, we decided to go swimming. It was hot, the sun was shining, and the nice, cool water would feel especially good.

We grabbed our towels, a bar of soap (might as well have a bath while there), and walked to the river. We had put on old pairs of cut-offs, and some old t-shirts, and were all ready to jump in.

"Oof," Sallie spluttered, as she headed for the deepest pool. "The water is *COLD*. I don't think Cyndi should come in, she'll freeze."

"I can too go in," Cyndi replied. "I'm a big girl now, and I like cold water."

She followed Sallie into the river but didn't get far before she was gasping and heading back to the shore.

Not to be outdone by her younger sister, Suzie followed Sallie into the deepest pool. Even though Suzie was looking uncomfortable, nothing would make her complain!

Sallie was squatting down in the water, thinking if she got herself completely wet, it would feel warmer. She was splashing water around and seemed to be enjoying herself.

In the meantime, Suzie started moving, but noticed a large, dark object that seemed to be following her ... she could not get away from it. With a gigantic leap, she landed smack dab in Sallie's arms. Sallie was standing there, holding Suzie, with a stunned look on her face.

"What are you doing?" Sallie asked, as she not-so-gently put Suzie back on her feet.

"There was a big, black thing following me. I think it's a whale," Suzie said. "I had to get away and there you were!"

"Suzie, look over there," Sallie said. "That big black thing is your shadow. See, I have one, too. It won't hurt you."

When I quit laughing, I made sure the girls got the bar of soap and made at least a pretense of washing themselves, before we returned to the cabin.

We made several more swimming trips to the river, but always warned Suzie ahead of time about her shadow.

CHAPTER 33

Often, the girls and I would grab the .22 single-shot rifle and go rabbit hunting. Rabbits were plentiful, and if we tired of eating them fried or roasted, I would grind them up to make "bunnyburgers."

Suzie and Sallie took turns shooting. They would connect with about two out of every three rabbits they aimed for.

One day I spotted a rabbit.

"Look over there," I whispered, "there sits a rabbit."

It was Suzie's turn to shoot the rabbit. However, Sallie was carrying the .22. Instead of handing the gun to Suzie, she aimed and fired. And, the rabbit fell over.

"Good shot," I said. "Go get it, and we'll see if we can find at least one more."

Sallie stood there looking bewildered, but finally she handed the gun to Suzie and made her way in the direction of the rabbit. She kept wandering around, looking befuddled, until I finally took pity on her and started giving her directions. Soon, she stumbled on the rabbit and picked it up triumphantly.

Stan and I were surprised that we didn't find a bullet hole in the rabbit when we skinned it. We concluded that the bullet must have just gone over its head, and the concussion killed it. (It was many months later that Sallie admitted she had not seen the rabbit when she shot. No wonder she had so much difficulty retrieving it.)

A few days later, we were once again out hunting, and this time Cyndi brought along her BB gun. She was about three years old at the time, and we did not let her have any BB's for her gun.

We spotted a rabbit, and Suzie was aiming, when suddenly, Cyndi cocked her BB gun and pulled the trigger. The rabbit heard the sound and was gone like a flash.

We all looked at Cyndi with shocked looks on our faces. She was very excited about "shooting" the rabbit and wanted to go get it. We had to explain to her that there was more to shooting a rabbit than pointing a gun and clicking the trigger (even though that worked for Sallie!) She never again spoiled a shot.

CHAPTER 34

Troop had gone to his reward and so had Red Dog. We were on the second or third generation of dogs. Sam, a yellow lab, had replaced Troop. Jeffery was a beagle we had given to Cyndi as a birthday present. He was mostly black, but had some brown spots; the most notable were the brown spots over his eyes. When we were at the cabin we still had our traditional sourdough pancakes for breakfast. The dogs loved the left-over pancakes. Or, so we believed.

Rose enjoying sourdough pancakes

I am not sure that the following is true. But, the girls have sworn on a stack of bibles that it is. They said they saw Jeffery take a whole pancake, haul it to the bridge over Wilbur Creek, and toss it into the creek. Now, does that sound like something any self-respecting dog that loved pancakes would do?

Speaking of Jeffery, he was a beagle that never learned from many hard lessons. He could not leave the porcupines alone. When he came in the door of the cabin, and raced under the bed, we knew that he had tangled with a porcupine once again. We had to get out the pliers, and de-quill him. We had a quart jar full of his "collection."

Sam, on the other hand, came home only once with one quill stuck in his nose. He never again tangled with a porcupine.

We still spent a good bit of time picking berries when we were at the mine. One day, as we were getting ready to go berry picking, Sallie asked, "Would it be all right if I fished instead of picked berries? I really like fishing better."

Thinking that a good mess of grayling would taste great, I agreed.

She was successful in catching enough fish for breakfast. From then on, she never went berry picking. She always stopped at the river with her fishing pole. Suzie loved to pick berries, so she would join the rest of us picking berries. We had both bases covered.

CHAPTER 35

One winter we let our old partner, Curt, stay in our cabin. We had a challenging time in the spring trying to get him to move out of the cabin. Apparently, he thought spending the winter gave him claim to the cabin. One day when he had gone to Fairbanks, we just moved his belongings over to Pete's house, and he was no longer living in our cabin.

When we moved his belongings, we missed a few things he had stashed in obscure areas. Over the years, they kept turning up. One such place was a shelf over the kitchen window where we found several items. There was a long cylinder that neither Stan nor I noticed. As the girls grew older, they spent more and more time at the cabin by themselves. We told them not to touch anything they didn't recognize, since we had no idea what he might have left behind. That may have been asking too much of inquisitive girls.

Stan and I were at the mine one afternoon when Sallie came running up, with tears streaming down her face.

"What happened," I asked. "Why are you crying?"

"Oh Mom," she said, "I know you told us not to touch anything we didn't recognize, but there was this long black thing over the kitchen window, and we wanted to see what it was. I don't know what happened, but it made a sort of 'swish' and then our eyes just started to smart and we were all crying. Suzie stayed with Cyndi outside, and I came to get you."

We shut down the pump and quickly made our way to the cabin. The whole cabin reeked. Neither Stan nor I had ever had any experience with tear gas, but we figured that was what had been in that cylinder. Our eyes were red and weeping, too, by the time we got the windows all opened and started to air out the cabin. We spent the night in Pete's house. I will say the girls never bothered playing with any cylinders after that.

CHAPTER 36

Sallie had a habit of sleep walking. We had to watch her closely so she didn't escape out the door and just disappear in the night. One time when we lived in North Pole and Cyndi was about seven-months old, I woke up hearing Cyndi crying. Then I heard our back-door close.

I jumped out of bed, and raced to the back door. There, just inside the door, stood a now wide-awake Sallie, with Cyndi in her arms. Cyndi was not a happy camper. She was hollering at the top of her lungs. Apparently, Sallie had closed the door behind her as she was bringing Cyndi back into the house. I must have been awfully tired, since I usually heard when any of the kids moved, let alone if they went outside!

Since it was about minus 20°F, it hadn't take Cyndi long to wake up and start crying. I was amazed to think that Sallie could have unlocked the back door and made her way outside without wakening either Stan or me! Coming back with a crying child did the trick.

After that, I considered putting a bell on her that would wake me when she was doing her antics, but I never did. I just tried to be more vigilant.

She had several episodes of sleep-walking when we were at the mine. Most of the time I would head her off and get her back to bed. But one time was unforgettable. Stan was with us at the mine since he'd taken the whole month of August off from work. We had quite a few hours of darkness since it was late in August.

We had gone to bed at a reasonable time. It was about four o'clock in the morning when Sallie sprang out of bed, and began racing around the kitchen table, yelling, "Fire! Fire!"

I realized right away that she was sleep walking but Stan didn't. He waked from a deep sleep, and when he heard her yell, he jumped over me and raced towards the kitchen. Soon he was in the dark kitchen, yelling too!

"Ouch, oh, Ouch!" he yelled.

I turned on the flashlight to see if I could figure out what was going on. Stan was holding his foot and hopping around on one leg. Sallie was cradling my red bathrobe in her arms and looked like a deer in the headlights.

"What happened?" I asked.

"I stubbed my toe when I went to put out the fire." Stan said. "And, there is no fire! It's just one of Sallie's crazy tricks. I ought to paddle her behind, but I don't suppose she knew what she was doing."

I got my bathrobe from Sallie and hung it back where it belonged. When Stan had started yelling, it woke Sallie up, and she was very confused. We got her back to bed, and we all tried to settle down for a good night's sleep. My problem was that the more I thought about the episode, the funnier it became, and I was soon snickering, but trying hard to stifle myself.

"Are you laughing?" Stan asked in a rather perturbed voice.

That did it, and I burst out in loud laughter. He was unamused. But, we finally did settle down and got back to sleep.

Stan's big toe turned black and blue and was painful for a week or so. Fortunately, Sallie never did warn us of fire again.

Stan and Mom enjoy a game

Stan relaxes on the couch

CHAPTER 37

One other incident happened around that time; it seemed very funny at the time, but maybe not so funny in retelling. It was a memorable experience, at least for Sallie. Suzie and Sallie had gotten old enough that we allowed them to ride in the back of the Weps when we drove it somewhere. There were benches along the side of the pickup box, but they preferred other seating. We had one folding camp chair. It had an aluminum frame, and a canvas seat.

The girls loved that chair, and would take turns sitting on it. They did not like sitting on the bench, so the one whose turn it wasn't for the chair would grab a water can to sit on.

It was Suzie's turn to sit on the canvas chair on this day. However, Sallie raced into the back of the Weps beating her to the chair. She plopped her behind in the chair with a smirk on her face. Sadly, she plopped down so hard the canvas seat ripped from one end to the other, dumping her on the floor. Her smirk soon turned to a look of astonishment as she realized what had happened.

Suzie burst into laughter, and both Stan and I may have had a chuckle at Sallie's misfortune. However, that was the last time there was any argument about whose turn it was to sit on that chair!

CHAPTER 38

When we first moved onto the mining claims we'd found several items that we did not recognize. They were four-feet long, and rounded. They looked so strange, sort of like half-barrels, but what were they?

When we went to Livengood for the mail, we'd asked John what they were.

"They are tailings directors," he told us. "You put them at the end of your slice box, and they carry the tailings away from your sluice. Otherwise, you just have a big pile of tailings, and you have to continually shovel it down to keep sluicing."

We hadn't needed them for many years, since we were not sluicing that much gravel. So, they lay piled up in various parts of the mining claims.

"I think we ought to try out those tailings directors," Stan said to me one morning as we were getting ready to sluice.

"I believe you're right," I replied. "If they work the way John described, they would sure save you a lot of work with the dozer, traveling constantly from the top of the sluice box to the bottom."

When Stan stacked the tailings with the dozer, he made a large pit at the end of the box. This soon filled with tailings when we started sluicing again. Once that pit filled, we could start laying out the tailings directors and direct the tailings to a different area.

Once we had them all laid out, we would begin removing them from the end, one at a time. They worked like a charm most of the time, and, with their aid, we could "direct" the tailings a long way away from the sluice box. However, the job of watching the tailings directors was a rough one.

If the tailings directors were not on a good water grade, they would jam up. Once they started jamming, it wasn't long before the tailings were not moving in the sluice box, and we had a major back-up problem.

One day my brother Henry (who had graduated from chef school, and was working in Fairbanks but staying at our house in North Pole) came to visit us at the mine.

"Is there anything I can do to help?" he asked.

"You sure can," I replied. "Grab that shovel, and see if you can keep the tailings directors from clogging up."

He obediently got the shovel, and was doing an exceptional job, until Stan brought in a dozer load of muddy, soupy gravel to the head of the sluice box. It flowed down through the sluice box like one big turd, without sluicing, and plugged up in the tailings directors. Henry took one look at the mess, and raced for the Black Shack, a little shack we had nearby that was our break shack. He never lived that one down.

As the girls got older, it became their job to direct the tailings. They got quite good at it, most of the time. One day they had a clog, and were blaming each other. I was aghast when I saw one of them throw a shovel at the other one. Stan was helping them at the time, trying to get the gravel in the tailings directors moving again, and saw the near hit. He scolded the girls soundly, and then sent them up to the giant to see their mother.

"All right, girls," I said. "What are you fighting about?"

Sallie replied, "Well, she started it. If she had just shoveled that gravel a little faster, we would not have that big jam."

Suzie, not to take this lying down, hollered. "No, it was all her fault. She's the one that caused that mess."

"O.K., girls," I said. "This is what I want you to do; kiss and make up."

"No way!" they both yelled. "I am *NOT* going to kiss her!"

"Oh, yes you are," I replied. And, I started to stand up to enforce my decision.

They unwillingly kissed each other and then went back to the tailings. Peace had been restored in the tailings director area, but now, every time I looked at them, I saw them whispering and giving me dirty looks. I felt lucky to get away with my scalp intact. I had united them against a common enemy, *ME*!

A small clog starting, but Sallie and Suzie still speaking

Tailings directors take a lot of work. Here, Suzie and
Sallie supervise as the sluicing continues

Time to relax when the directing goes as it should

Stan's Aunt Gertrude learns to pan from instructions
offered by Cyndi

CHAPTER 39

We decided one Christmas to buy the girls a horse for their present. We found this young Appaloosa mare at a local riding school, and bought her as a gift for all three girls. We could board her at the riding school until summer when Stan would build a barn. The fun part of the deal was Suzie and Sallie could have riding lessons the rest of the winter.

They got their riding lessons, and in the spring, Stan built a beautiful barn on our North Pole property. He made it large enough that we could have three horses, rabbit cages, a chicken coop, and even a pen for pigs if we so desired. The girls were very happy when they could get their horse, Winona, home and volunteered to take care of her every day, which, they did.

Soon it was time to move to the mine for the summer.

"I saw an ad for wiener pigs for sale, and I think we should get a couple." Stan said. "We can also get some laying hens, and some day-old chicks; maybe some geese, ducks, turkeys, and a guinea or two. We can convert the back cabin into a barn, and I'll build a pig pen near the machine shed. And, we can leave the chicks in the barn with Winona."

"Wow, you have been thinking," I replied. "I guess we can do all that. We need to hire someone to haul Winona to the mine anyway, and I think we could haul the rest in the International." (The International was the one that my sister dubbed the Grey Ghost.)

All went according to Stan's plan. We found a trucker that hauled Winona to the mine in his horse trailer, and the pigs (Waldo and Wertha) and chickens moved with us.

Once at the mine, Winona was very friendly, and very much a "people horse." One day I had the door open into the garage, when I heard, "clomp, clomp, clomp."

I looked up and imagine my surprise to see Winona entering the door. Sallie grabbed her, led her around the barrel stove located in the middle of the room, and back outside. From then on, when I had the door open, I put a chair in the doorway to keep her out.

We did not need to picket Winona. She would go off to eat but would always show up at 4:30 pm. Occasionally, she would wander up to the mine where Stan was working. She seemed to prefer drinking the muddy water coming from the mine cut, instead of the water in the creek.

One day when she was having a drink from the mine water, Stan decided he'd jump on her back and ride her home. Of course, he was without saddle and bridle.

Sallie had not thought to tell Stan that Winona was afraid of puddles. I looked out the window just in time to see Stan flying past on Winona headed for the barn. Fortunately, the gate to the corral was closed, or he might have been decapacitated going through the barn door! Being nosy, I wondered what was going on. I went to investigate.

"What are you doing?" I asked. "Why were you on Winona, and why were you going so fast?"

"You wouldn't believe what that fool horse did," he replied, shakily. "We were trotting along just fine, headed home, until we came to that little puddle by the duck pond. Then, she just bolted, and it was all I could do to hang on and not get thrown. I'm going to teach her a lesson."

Stan got her bridle and saddle, and then made her walk carefully through the shallow pond repeatedly. He was finally satisfied, but it didn't seem to make much difference to Winona. She still bolted at puddles.

Summer waned and it was time to butcher the pigs. One morning Stan rigged up a pole, so he could lower them into a barrel of boiling water to scald; this was necessary so he could scrape the bristles off the hide. He had the first pig scalded and was removing the intestines, when I found Cyndi sitting on a hill, crying her eyes out.

"What's the matter?" I asked.

"Dad shot Waldo," she wailed, "and he put him in hot water!"

Recalling how she was so enthralled with finding un-laid eggs in some of the hens when we butchered them, I said, "Do you suppose Waldo will have pig eggs?"

Her eyes dried immediately, and began to shine, and she asked, "Do you really think so?" I told her, "Anything is possible." She was off like a streak before I could say anything further.

When Stan finished the butchering, and came in the house, he said, "What did you say to Cyndi? She left me bawling, and then, before I knew what she was up to, she was elbow deep inside the pig looking for something."

Unfortunately, she never did find the pig eggs, but not for lack of trying.

Waldo and Wertha

My Mom with the chickens

CHAPTER 40

"Would you girls like to learn to drive?" Stan asked one morning. Suzie and Sallie were teenagers and would soon be old enough to get their driver's licenses. Driving from the cabin to the river would give them practice, and there was no traffic.

"We sure would," they both replied. So, he set off with both in the Weps. Sallie picked it up almost immediately, but Suzie had trouble. She couldn't get the clutch to work and would kill the engine almost every time she tried to take off. Then, she would give it so much gas that when she let the clutch out, she would lurch off at a neck-jerking pace.

Lessons continued for nearly a month. During that time, Sallie became more proficient, but Suzie continued to struggle, including smacking into the wood pile, and running over a tree stump.

"I think maybe we should wait for Suzie to take driver's education in school," Stan said one morning. "I'm not doing very well at teaching her to drive."

So, while we still offered Suzie the opportunity to drive when we were headed for the river, she usually refused.

"I think Sallie is doing well enough to drive the Grey Ghost." Stan said one morning. This was our 1965 International Panel Truck.

The Grey Ghost, with the Rybachek family

Sallie was very excited. She loved anything new and had been begging to drive the Ghost for quite some time.

Sallie and Stan headed for the river in the Ghost. In about half an hour I saw them both walking back up the hill to the cabin.

"What happened?" I asked. "Where's the Gray Ghost?"

"We had a problem," Stan replied. "I told her she could shift from low gear into second, and instead she hit reverse. The transmission is out of the Gray Ghost, and it's parked right in the middle of the road."

This was a rather startling incidence. I had been wanting to get rid of the Ghost for some time, but perhaps not this way. Fortunately, we had the Weps at the mine, so had transportation, and we could drag the Ghost back to the yard. Which we did.

Stan went to town a few days later with plans to look for parts for the transmission. Instead, he came home in a 1975 Ford F250. While it didn't have an enclosed area like the panel had, it was a great truck and gave us many years of service. I was not sure if I should congratulate Sallie for getting us a new truck, or smack her behind!

Our new Red Truck

Stan takes the lazy way home, riding Goliath

Goliath wistfully looks for some grain

CHAPTER 41

We bought the girls two more horses the next spring. We bought a Morgan gelding for Cyndi, named Goliath; and a Quarter-horse for Suzie, whose name was Stormy's Vaquero, but his nickname was "Vacca."

Goliath   Vacca

After all, Stan *had* built three stalls in the barn. We had quite a time getting our menagerie to the mine that summer. (See Bumps in the Road, by Rose Rybachek, 2015, Chapter 28).

Cyndi plays with Jim and John

We had, not only the three horses, but also two more pigs (Jim and John), several rabbits, two geese, two ducks, our laying hens, and two dogs. Our treks to the mine were getting complicated.

The girls spent quite a bit of time barrel racing the Morgan, since he was trained for that.

Cyndi and Goliath do barrel jumps

They went on long rides using some of the old mining trails. They picketed the horses each day so they would have fresh grass. They found that if they picketed Goliath, the other horses would stay with him until evening.

Winona continued her habit of coming home when it was 4:30 pm, so usually the girls would wait until she showed up, then ride her back to the picket area to retrieve the other two horses.

Winona

CHAPTER 42

Stan decided one day that he would cool his afternoon beer in the creek. He made a little nest alongside the bank, added some beer and sodas for the girls.

He was very upset when he went to get his beer, and it was not there. He thought it strange the creek would be selective and take away his beer, leaving the sodas. The next day he again brought beer to cool, and once again the beer disappeared, leaving behind the sodas. He knew it was just too much of a coincidence that his beer would disappear like that, while the sodas remained.

Stan was convinced that the girls had been pilfering his beer. "Did you girls steal my beer?" he angrily asked them, "come on, tell me. I promise I won't be mad," he shouted.

"You're already mad," Sallie replied, "but we didn't have anything to do with it, honest."

The next day the same thing happened. That time the girls were still busy doing chores at the cabin, and had not even been to the mining operation.

"I can't figure it out," Stan said. "What's happening to my beer?"

The following day he kept a watchful eye on his beer stash. Imagine his surprise to see Sam walk over to the little dam, dunk his head under the water, and come up with a can of beer. He trotted over behind a tailings pile and set the can down gingerly. Then, he punched a hole in the side with his teeth, and lapped the spurting beer as quickly as he could. When the fizz quit, he headed back towards the dam for another one. He had quite a stash of partially empty beer cans behind the tailings pile. He had no soda cans!

"Hey, you are *NOT* getting away with any more of my beer," Stan yelled, as he headed Sam off from a refill. The next day Stan brought a five-gallon bucket to the mine, filled it with water, and put his beer in that, along with the sodas.

Would you believe our beer-loving dog fished the beer out of the bucket! Stan tried putting the beer under the sodas with only partial luck. He finally put a large rock in the bucket on top of the beer, and that was the end of the pilfering.

CHAPTER 43

We were visited often by family and friends from the lower 48. One-year Stan's brother Ralph visited from Chicago. "I think I'm going to let Ralph pan some gravel today," Stan said one morning. "You have a jar with gold in it, don't you? We'll salt his pan with a half-ounce or so of gold, and he'll have it to show his friends when he gets home."

Ralph was excited to think that he was going to learn to pan. "I don't know the first thing about it," he said. "You'll have to show me everything."

I tagged along with them, just to watch as Stan showed Ralph the fine art of panning. We had a small puddle near the giant that we used for panning our samples. Stan upended a five-gallon bucket near the pond, and got a nice pan of gravel. I watched as he stealthily added the gold. We were about as excited as Ralph was, thinking of how thrilled he would be when the gold started showing.

For those that have never panned, gold is much heavier than rocks or sand, and you very seldom see any gold until you have gotten all of the gravel and most of the sand washed away.

Stan showed Ralph how he panned. Ralph sat on the bucket and panned. He kept looking closely at the pan.

When he was getting down to mostly just sand left in the pan, he suddenly stood up, and flung the contents of the pan as far as he could toss it.

"Skunked!" he exclaimed in disgust.

Stan and I stood there with our mouths wide open. We knew that he had just tossed a good half ounce of gold out on the ground.

"I want to try another pan." Ralph said.

"Well, okay," Stan said, "but next time, you need to pan in a wash tub." And he did. After he left to back home, we re-sluiced the area of his toss.

Ralph pans in the wash tub

CHAPTER 44

Stan had to work most of the summer of 1978. Suzie had just graduated from high school and Sallie had just finished her junior year. The girls and I lived at the mine. I kept the face washed, so when Stan would take his vacation in August, we would have gravels thawed so we could sluice them.

It was my habit to go up to the mine twice a day, in the morning and in the evening, if we had enough water. I had been doing that for the month of June and into July. I usually went up after dinner while the girls did the dishes.

We were just finishing dinner one Thursday evening when there was a very authoritative knock on our door. I went to the door, not knowing what to expect. I considered picking up the pistol on my way, since the knock had nearly shaken the door off its hinges. But, I decided that might not be "polite," and I didn't want to stoop to the rudeness of the person knocking.

I opened the door, and there was no one there. So, I looked around the door into the yard and saw someone standing in the yard. I ventured out the door. There were three men standing there, each wearing a side arm.

"Ma'am," the one who appeared to be the boss said, "We are here from the Department of Environmental Conservation. Is your husband home?"

"Well, no, he isn't," I replied. "He should be back tomorrow evening. Can you tell me why you want him?"

"We just want to talk to him about muddy water," the man replied. "We will be back."

With that, they turned and walked out of the yard. I went back in the house and finished my dinner. When I figured enough time had elapsed for them to be out of earshot, I went up and washed the face like I usually did.

I expected them to show up on Friday night, but they didn't. Stan and I talked it over when he arrived on Friday evening and decided that the best defense was to play dumb. I was well equipped to do that.

A week went by, and again, the girls and I were eating dinner on a Thursday evening when we heard a loud knock on the door. When I went outside, there were the same three guys standing there with their side arms. Again, the leader asked, "Is your husband home?"

"No," I replied again. "I expect he'll be back tomorrow evening. Can I help you?"

"No," he replied. "I need to talk to your husband. We will return."

I almost said, "thanks for the warning," but managed to curb my tongue. And as before, I finished my dinner, and washed the face, as per my habit.

It was getting to be tiresome when a few days later, we were again having our dinner, and there was a loud knock on the door.

It was the same three men again, and once more they didn't want to talk to me. I was happy to see them walk down the road. And again, I finished my dinner, and went to wash the face. It was almost the first of August, and in a few days Stan would have his vacation. We hoped to get some sluicing done.

Stan and I both were rather worried that those three men might return while we were sluicing. We worried they might cause us delay.   but that was the last we saw or heard of them.

The Hector Sluice box was a 3-channel box, with water automatically feeding the gravels

CHAPTER 45

We had heard great reports about the Hector Sluice Box. One advantage was that you hooked it to your pipeline, and then you didn't have to use the giant to wash the gravels down the box. It fed itself.

"I think we ought to buy one of those Hector Boxes," Stan said. "You wouldn't have to sit there all the time running the giant, and I can teach you how to run the dragline. I can use the D-8 to stack the gravel, and Cyndi can feed the box with the front-end loader."

"You think I can actually learn to run the dragline?" I asked. We had acquired a small two-yard dragline several years before. It had taken Stan a couple of weeks before he was proficient. Could I ever learn?

"I've seen you up there, using both feet and both hands," I continued. "It looks awfully complicated to me."

"It looks harder than it really is," Stan said. "I'll give you your first lesson next week when just you and I are at the mine and then you won't have an audience while you're learning."

He ordered the Hector sluice box and had it delivered to the mine site. It took a bit of work to get it set up and the plumbing connected, but we did it. And he did give me operating lessons for the dragline. I was not nearly as coordinated as he was, and it took me a lot longer than his estimated two weeks before I felt comfortable getting that bucket near enough to the sluice box to remove the tailings. However, we were soon ready to start sluicing.

Rose operating dragline

Stan showed Cyndi how to operate the front-end loader, and we were all lined up to do our various jobs. Stan brought in a large load of gravel, and Cyndi attacked it with the loader. I called her my FELO, which stood for Front-End Loader Operator.

Betsy, our front-end loader

She started off doing well, but soon she didn't give the loader enough gas, and the engine stalled. She got it started again and that time gave it too much gas, and she ended up with about a teaspoon in the bucket, but the engine was roaring. After a while, Stan had to park the dozer and feed some gravel into the sluice box himself. He showed her how to do it again, and she was on her own once more.

The same thing happened again, and Stan had to come rescue her. After about a week of this, Stan finally said to me, "I think I can handle both jobs. I'll just work-up a stock pile of gravel after we shut down and you're cooking dinner. Then I can run the loader until the stockpile is gone. When you go to cook lunch, I can make another stockpile. We can let Cyndi retire."

Poor Cyndi, she was no longer my FELO, dismissed in disgrace. But I think she was much happier at the cabin. In the meantime, I was learning how to operate the dragline, and most of my tailings piles passed inspection. I only dinged the sluice box a couple of times.

Rose at the helm of the dragline

It was time for a new dozer since the old one developed final drive problems. Stan found a good deal on one, and had it delivered. (See Bumps in the Road, by Rose Rybachek, 2015, Chapter 33). He was very proud of his "new" dozer.

Stan and his new dozer

CHAPTER 46

We still had Sam, our yellow Labrador, but we lost Jeffrey and had a new Yorkie mix named Hannibal. Sam loved sticks, and retrieving them. When he saw a stick that had fallen from the row of vegetation about fifteen-foot off the gravel, his eyes would glow like the Hound of the Baskerville's. Sam also loved fighting with the water coming from the giant when we were first turning it on. In the early 1970s, we had converted from using gravity to pressure the giant to using a pump. Sam could hardly wait for the water to appear once he heard the pump start.

Sam waiting for the water, while Hannibal watches

Sam seemed to believe the water was his arch-nemesis that threatened his sticks.

His mission was to save as many sticks as possible from the evil water.

Sam saves one stick from the water

Is it going to get him?

"Have you noticed that huge pile of sticks Sam drug up from in front of the face?" Stan said one morning at breakfast. "I keep worrying about him when he goes under that overhang to get another stick. I've seen some quite large chunks fall, and he got splattered quite badly just yesterday. Besides, he's making his stockpile right in front of the drag line, and when we need to move the dragline, his stack of wood is going to be in the way."

Sam had a huge stockpile of sticks he had piled near the dragline. Some of the sticks were so heavy he couldn't lift them, but instead had to drag them, tugging and tugging to get them away from the face.

Sam retrieving sticks

"I need to move the dragline," Stan said to me a few days later. "The gravel pile is getting too high and I can't stack much more on it."

Stan took the D-8 and made a nice pad on which to park the dragline. Unfortunately for Sam, the new parking spot was behind his stockpile. I was afraid he was going to get run over as he tried valiantly to move his stockpile before Stan got the sticks all buried. He did a credible job, too, but many ended up buried.

Stan got the dragline moved but Sam didn't come home for a few nights. He stayed up at the mine mourning the loss of his stick pile.

One-day Cyndi tossed a stick into the sluice box. Sam dived right into the box to rescue it. He caught it before it reached the end. Cyndi soon tired of sending Sam down the sluice box, so she tossed the next stick up on the catwalk of the dragline. Sam was baffled. He could see it, but couldn't figure out how to get it. Cyndi finally went over to the dragline, jumped up on the track, then into the cab and walked down the catwalk to retrieve the stick.

The next time she tossed the stick on the catwalk for Sam, he jumped on the track, then into the cab and turned around and then down the catwalk. He retrieved his stick, then backed all the way down the catwalk into the cab, then jumped down on the track, and took the stick to Cyndi to throw for him again. We were all flabbergasted that after one lesson, he had figured out how to retrieve his stick. Wonder how he would have done learning to run the front-end-loader?

CHAPTER 47

I had taken a job with KTVF, one of the local TV stations. One of my friends at work had a cat with a litter of kittens, so I decided I would surprise Cyndi with a cute little kitten.

"Cyndi," I said to her. "How would you like a kitten? My friend at work has a litter of little kittens, and you can pick one out. Then when its old enough, we can bring it home."

"Can I really have a kitten?" Cyndi replied."

"Sure," I said. "Let's go."

We went to my friend's house, and Cyndi picked out a young male kitten that was white and orange colored. She was thrilled when he was big enough to bring home. I was quite surprised when we got him, to find he had rather long hair. I really did not want a long- haired cat, but I could not break my promise.

Trying to find an unusual name for him, we stumbled across information about a Herkimer Diamond. Apparently, the Herkimer Diamond is a rare form of quartz, but it also might have mystical properties.

That seemed like the perfect name for this little bundle of fur. Herkimer, he was.

Herkimer lived up to his name. He was an unusual kitten and liked to ride in cars. He would sit on the driver's lap, put his two front paws on the steering wheel, and be happy to "steer" for a long time.

He also didn't mind baths and would often jump in the bathtub with whoever was having a bath.

He only had one drawback. He decided he was MY cat and always followed me around. He was very unhappy when I left. Sometimes when I took a trip, he would ignore me for ten days, or two weeks after I returned. Then he would be friends again.

He had a habit of gently chewing on a person's chin when he liked that person. I got lots of "chin jobs" when I was in his good graces. I missed that when he was holding a grudge.

He was a very successful hunter. One time when he was just a little kitten, he got lost at the mine. The girls found him the next morning sitting beside a pile of entrails. He had apparently enjoyed his dinner.

He usually ate whatever he caught, but, one day when we were staying at the mine, he deposited a fully-grown, dead weasel on the porch. At the mine cabin, he had a secret passage way so he could get in and out. We left him plenty of food and water if we left him alone there.

Herkimer

Cyndi was not very happy with her cat, and his misplaced affection, so when her bus driver offered her another cat, she was ready to "trade". Thus, JD also came into our lives.

JD was also a special cat. He was an indoor cat, and the only time he'd been outside was when his mistress took him for a walk on a leash. He knew nothing about being a real cat. But, he was Cyndi's.

Moving to the mine presented a challenge with our two cats. We ended up putting JD into a box, and he howled the entire trip. But we arrived safely. Cyndi carried the box into the cabin and opened the lid. JD leaped out and raced into the kitchen.

This was the first time we'd been at the cabin for months, and a horde of mice had moved in. Mice were running every which way. JD pounced, and soon had a mouse under each front foot, plus one in his mouth. Then, a rather vacant look came into his eyes.

He gingerly sat the mouse down that was in his mouth and watched as it scampered away. Next to go was the one under his right foot, and that one, too, scampered away. Finally, he lifted his left foot and let that one loose. We were all standing there, in shock!

Herkimer, on the other hand, had raced in, caught one mouse, and was busily eating his catch. He didn't wait for the dinner bell or anything, just happily had dinner.

With the cats in the house, the mice made themselves scarce, and we never saw them again, during that stay. They would wait until we left and then move back in.

CHAPTER 48

Stan said to me one morning, "What do you think about applying for a patent? I was talking with a guy from the Bureau of Land Management office the other day, and he thinks it's going to get more and more difficult to get a patent. I think if we're ever going to get one, we'd better get busy now!"

"I agree," I replied. "We need to get the information and see just what we need to do to qualify."

The next time we were in town, we stopped by the Bureau of Land Management (BLM), picked up the information, and talked with a couple of the geologists. The discussion ended with them telling us that we would have to drill a certain number of holes on the claims. And drilling through permafrost could be expensive.

"You know," Stan said on our way back to the cabin. "I was talking to someone at the last Miner's meeting, and he mentioned that there's a place in Oklahoma that specializes in selling used churn drills.

I bet if we had one we could do our own drilling, and all we'd have to do is have BLM come up to sample when we hit gravel."

Upon further investigation, and talking with the BLM Geologists again, the plan was fleshed out. We contacted the place in Oklahoma, and they had churn drills for sale. They agreed they would mount one on a truck for us. It would be ready around the middle of January, and we could pick it up in Oklahoma. We were happy to have an excuse to leave Alaska in the winter. Suzie and Sallie had both graduated from high school, and were off on their own but Cyndi was in 6th grade.

January saw us finally put our red Ford Pickup on the ferry in Haines. I say "finally" because we had one heck of a time getting to Haines. We ran into white-out conditions before we got to Haines Junction. The wind was howling and the snow was blowing sideways. We decided to spend the night at a motel in Haines Junction. It was located next door to a package store that sold alcoholic beverages.

There was black ice all over. While Cyndi and I were sitting in the truck, waiting for Stan to make the arrangements for the motel room, we saw a "gentleman" exit from the package store with a sack-covered bottle in his hand. As he came down the steps, he slipped on the ice. His feet flew out from under him, and he started sliding on his rear. The last we saw of him, as he disappeared into the darkness, he was carefully holding his bottle high so it didn't get broken on his trip down the road.

Anyway, we gingerly made our way to our room and had a good night. We left on the last leg of our journey to Haines the next morning. It was about a hundred and fifty miles away. The visibility was poor, and the wind was still blowing snow, so it was a harrowing trip. We were happy they had planted large poles with reflectors along the edge of the road, or we might have been forever in a snowbank.

We got the pickup onboard the ferry for Seattle, got settled in our tiny stateroom, and Cyndi and I went exploring. As we went out a door (or was it a hatch?) onto the deck, the whistle blew. We were right under it and we both hit the deck. We thought we had been shot, for sure. We were very happy when it quit blowing and we were still intact. That was a shocker.

We had a delightful trip on the ferry. We even got to meet some friends of ours in Ketchikan, plus we toured the town. We had heard so much about Ketchikan, but this was our first visit. Sitka was another exciting town to see with all the Russian influence and architecture. But when we landed in Seattle, we found they were experiencing an ice storm. We felt fortunate that the pickup had four-wheel-drive.

It was another anxious trip to find the airport. My Mom was flying from Montana to meet us there and would continue our trip with us, all the way to back to Alaska. My Dad passed away in 1978. Since Mom was alone, she started spending more time with us and would spend most summers with us at the mine. We were always happy to have her, as she was great company.

In Seattle, our route seemed to lead only up-hill, and we had to stop at every cross road. Some cars were kitty-wampus in the road; once they got stopped, they could not get going again, and spun out. We had to weave our way in and out between the stalled traffic. Besides, we were not familiar with Seattle, and we had to hurry in order to meet Mom's plane. It was a nightmare.

Miracles do happen, however, and we found the airport in time to pick her up; then we headed down the coast. We visited with some of Stan's half-brothers and sisters along the way, spent a few days at Disneyland, and had a wonderful time. Crossing the white sands in New Mexico was another thrill for us. Soon we were in Oklahoma City, ready to pick up our truck, and head north.

Another disappointment loomed, because the truck was NOT ready to go. It took them a whole week of working on it before they thought it would make the trip to Alaska. The worst problem was with the lighting system. I still remember the mechanic (Punkin), as he worked to get the lights operable. He finally said they were ready to go, and while we did have lights that would turn on and off with the switch, they also had a few problems. For instance, the headlights would come on every time Stan put his foot on the brake. This could be a problem when going through weigh stations.   Stan solved that one by just driving with his lights on all the time.   He hoped that the battery would be strong enough to start the truck the next morning.

Another problem was every time Stan stepped on the brakes, the horn would honk.   That one was harder to camouflage, but no one ever questioned his honking.

View of the drill truck that Mom and I followed on our way to Alaska

Stan had installed CB radios in both the Red Truck that I was driving, and in the drill truck, that he was driving.   Cyndi rode with Stan, while Mom rode with me.

We had a few adventures along the way like getting lost in Calgary.   I had stopped for gas outside of Calgary, and had not caught up with Stan yet when he and Cyndi passed the sign for the road to Alaska. We were out of radio range since our radios only covered about five miles. Mom and I saw the sign for the road to Alaska, but it was small, and almost hidden in some bushes. We debated and finally decided the chances of Stan seeing that sign were slim, so we continued into the heart of Calgary. We had gone a short distance, when I was finally able to raise Stan on the radio, and sure enough, he was ahead of us.

"Where are you," I asked.

Through the static, I heard, "We are sitting at a park. The road dead-ended here, and we don't know where to go!"

We found them quickly, and calmed our nerves by eating a sandwich while trying to figure out from the maps how to get back on the right road. We had no GPS, but one surely would have come in handy. Unfortunately, they hadn't been invented yet.

We were very lucky in not finding any more dead-ends and were soon out of Calgary and on the road to Alaska. The further north we went, the colder it got. Stan turned on the defrosters one day, and instead of getting hot-air out of them, they spurted antifreeze. Not good at all! Not only did it make the windshield nearly impossible to see out, it also made the air in the cab of the truck noxious. They had to stop and clean off the windshield, and then drive with the windows down the rest of the day.

When we got to the motel that night, they were both nearly frozen and sick to their stomachs. Mom, Cyndi, and I thought the hot tub would feel particularly good, especially to Cyndi. We got on our swimsuits and went to the hot tub. We had barely gotten in it, when Cyndi passed out. Apparently, the hot water on top of breathing the anti-freeze fumes had her on the ropes. She revived by the time we got her back to the motel room but just wanted to go to sleep.

She seemed to be good to go the next morning, and the odor had almost gone from inside the cab of the truck. Although, Stan never again tried the defrosters. If the visibility got too bad, he would pull over and scrape the frost.

Then we started having trouble with the drill truck tires. Apparently, the tires they had put on the truck were nearly worn out, so they started going flat. The nails Stan kept picking up didn't help, either.

When we finally got to our house in North Pole we had two inside duals that were flat, but the outside duals were still holding. We were happy to arrive home safe and sound. Cyndi was not all that happy about having to go back to school, but she did.

Stan did not even try to use the drill that winter. He thought it would be wise to drill some holes the next summer near the cabin so he could learn to use the drill. And that is what he did. He drilled several holes and learned more tricks of the trade with each hole. By fall he was ready to think about how and when to drill for real. With the deep perma-frost on most of our mining claims, he would have to drill after the ground had frozen, and before it thawed out in the spring.

A practice hole in the back yard.
Barn and grain shed on right

CHAPTER 49

The BLM geologists drove to the mine in their pickup about mid-summer and helped Stan map out where he should drill the holes. While there, they did some sampling of various tailings piles. In one they found quite a bit of gold, so they were impressed. About two weeks later, they came back.

"We have the Assistant Secretary of the Interior coming to Alaska next week, and she wants to see how we conduct a mineral survey. Would it be all right if we brought her here?" they asked. "We can sample some of the gravel from that tailings pile that produced so well."

"Sure, I don't see why not," Stan said.

On the allotted day, they all arrived in several different vehicles. The geologists busied themselves getting set up to do the sample. They had a machine called an Easy Panner, that would process buckets of gravel, leaving the heavy materials in the small riffles. They could process larger amounts of gravel using that machine than just panning.

They dug out several buckets of gravel from the area that had been such a good producer and set about sluicing. We were all excited to see what they would find, and the Assistant Secretary was impressed with their professionalism.

Easy Panner

"I don't see a thing," one of the geologists said after they'd panned the gravel from the riffles. "Let's try over here, where we only got a few colors last time." They dug several more buckets of gravel and processed it.

"Skunked again," he said. "We can try one more time before we need to have lunch, and go back to town."

Well, as Murphy's Law says, whatever can go wrong will ... and sure enough, another dry hole. I am not sure the Assistant Secretary was overly impressed towards the end of their survey; it would have been much more impressive if they had found something. We fixed a lunch for the whole crew, which they enjoyed, and then we sat around in the cabin visiting. Soon they were on their way back to Fairbanks.

"I sure hope they have better luck when they sample the drill holes!" Stan said.

The next spring, it was time to begin the drilling program. He cleared an ice road to where he was to drill the first hole, got the drill in position, hauled the tank of water, and started his drilling. It took him about four days before he struck gravel. Then it was my job to go into town, and bring back the geologists.

We were quite shocked to see them pan the first time we hit gravel. They were not nearly as careful as we thought they should be. After that, we convinced them to pan in a washtub. When they left, we could pan it ourselves. In most instances, we could double their findings. Was that why they weren't able to impress the Assistant Secretary?

It took Stan two springs to get all the holes drilled, but the geologists never complained about coming out to do their investigation. Maybe the fresh cinnamon rolls helped! At the end of the period they wrote up their report, and found that we had claims rich enough for a prudent man to mine. This was a great finding for us, since we knew they didn't catch all the gold in their pans.

CHAPTER 50

We were busily mining, but it was moose season. Stan would get up early every morning to see if he could find a nice bull before we began our day's sluicing. One morning I heard a shot coming from the direction of the river.

When Stan came through the door I immediately asked, "Did you get him?"

"Well, yes and no," Stan replied. "I shot him, and he ran a few steps and then fell in the river. He floated down around the corner and lodged in a beaver dam. I think we can get the Weps and use the winch to retrieve him. We can't get too close because the beaver dam has water backed up, and it's pretty deep there."

We drove the Weps down to the beaver dam in the river after breakfast. There was the moose lodged in the dam with water flowing over most of him. His horns were sticking out quite well, though. Stan waded out in his hip boots to get close enough to the horns to wrap the cable around him and we pulled him to shore.

Stan immediately cleaned and skinned the critter. When skinning, Stan found three bullets lodged under his skin from previous encounters with hunters. The poor moose must have barely recovered, and was really tough; the meat grinder barely turned him into burger, but he was tasty.

A few days later we were awakened in the middle of the night by a vehicle driving into our yard. Imagine our surprise to see Sallie get out of her truck.

"What are you doing here in the middle of the night?" Stan asked.

"I have some bad news," she replied. "Remember how Grandma's ankle has been bothering her all summer? Well, she went to the doctor when she got back to Montana, and they found she has breast cancer. She will be having a mastectomy tomorrow. I just thought you should know."

We were on the road back to Fairbanks early the next morning. I managed to talk to Mom on the phone before she went into surgery. The surgery went well, and they got all the cancer. In addition, her ankle had a miraculous healing and never bothered her again.

CHAPTER 51

At the start of the mining season of 1980, Stan gave notice to his employer. We had decided to mine full time. The mine had proved that it could support us, and our future looked bright.

However, toward the end of the 1970's, and the early 1980's, the Environmental Protection Agency (EPA) started making its presence known in Alaska. With the passage of the Clean Water Act in 1972, the EPA argued that the water used in mining was a hazard to anadromous fish, especially the waste water produced by hydraulic mining.

In our opinion, they failed to consider the history of hydraulic mining, and the fact that the anadromous fish were thriving and had been for years. Unfortunately, they were not impressed by our opinion. There were roughly between 800 and 900 small Mom and Pop placer miners in Alaska at the time.

We were told at a meeting of miners that there had been a secret meeting in Seattle attended by the EPA, the National Park Service, BLM, and the IRS. Our informant said that he talked to an employee of the BLM who had attended the meeting, but did not want his name to be made public.

Our informant said, "Would you believe my friend told me that the group considered buying out all the active miners by condemning their property through eminent domain? They argued long and hard, and he said the BLM was the only agency in favor of the buy-out program. The other agencies favored tough enforcement to drive the miners out of business. They want to stop all placer mining in Alaska.

"The IRS was upset because it felt the miners would save their gold from year to year, and only sell what they needed in any given year. Thus, they could control the amount of income they had to pay tax on.

"The EPA was flexing its muscles and wanted to drive every miner off the land, while the National Park Service joined in with that plan.

"So, the final conclusion was that EPA would make it so expensive to treat placer mining wastewater that very few, if any, placer miners would be able to make a living. Before long, placer mining would be as dead as the Dodo bird. And, not one agency from the State of Alaska was invited to this secret meeting."

If this was true, it was not good news. We had spent a lot of money, time and effort developing our mine, not to mention the lengthy process of applying for the patent to the property. The patent was not issued yet, and if the agencies had agreed to put miners out of business, we might never get our patent. We were hydraulic mining, and had very limited room to build settling ponds. Our mining future suddenly looked bleak.

We joined several of the mining organizations to try to make our side of the story known. But, most of our pleas fell on deaf ears. It seemed to us that many of the "enforcers" were trying to see just which ones could be the most vicious in their enforcement.

We were thrilled in December of 1983, when we received the patent to the 255 acres of our mining property. I believe it was the last large patent issued in Alaska since that date. And, what a neat Christmas present.

In July of 1984, our friend Joe Vogler was hauling supplies to his mining claims on Woodchopper and Webber Creeks like he had done for years, driving his dozer along the Bielenberg Trail. He was stopped by an armed gang of rangers from the National Park Service, arriving in helicopters, and Joe was served with a restraining order.

When we saw Joe later that year we asked him about his "arrest."

"They were heavily armed," he said. "They had semi-automatic weapons, and side arms. And they were spoiling for a fight. They tried every way they could think of to make me mad enough to fight them. I'm convinced that if my friend hadn't flown over in his plane, and circled around where we were until they got me loaded in their helicopter, they would have killed me. As it was, they really tried to make me mad enough to fight back, but I didn't want to give them that satisfaction."

As far as I know, Joe's supplies never did get delivered, and his dozer and equipment are still rusting on the Bielenberg trail.

Chapter 52

We continued mining as usual. Since Suzie and Sallie had moved out of the house, we sold Winona and Vacca, but kept Goliath for Cyndi. We stopped raising pigs, but in the summer of 1984, we purchased two black calves that we were planning on fattening up and butchering in the fall.

Stan "drives" the steers to water, Goliath shows the way

During the latter part of the summer we had several fly-overs by a black helicopter. The chopper would circle the cabin several times, always tipped so that we could not read the number, if it had one.

Then, it would circle the sluice box in the same manner. We were very worried as to what the helicopter was up to, and who it belonged to. We had heard horror stories of miners that had their sluice boxes ripped off by persons unknown landing in a helicopter.

Fortunately, we were not sluicing yet, but we were getting the sluice box set and ready to go. We tried every way we could think of to read the number on that helicopter, including using binoculars, but the pilot was very adept at protecting it.

The first fly-over we experienced was in the late afternoon. When Cyndi went to bring her horse and the two calves home, she found that her horse had been spooked by something. He had gotten his picket chain wrapped around some willows, and was snubbed up tight. She could free him, but one of the calves was upside down in a water-filled depression, and she could not get him up. She had to find Stan to help her release him.

It took us a while to figure out what must have spooked our animals. Then, the light dawned. It was no doubt the helicopter doing its fly over. Thereafter, when we had a fly-over, one or the other of us would go check on the picketed critters to make sure they were all right. Sometimes they were, and sometimes they were not.

Stan and I were working on the sluice box at the mining operation, after at least two weeks of daily fly overs, when the helicopter landed. Getting out of it were six heavily armed men carrying semi-automatic rifles, plus wearing side arms and bright orange flak jackets. Four of them stayed with the helicopter, while the other two started walking in our direction. One followed the other about ten paces behind.

"Good afternoon," the leader said. "My name is Commodore Mann. I am with the EPA, and I'm here to inspect your settling ponds. Can you show me where they are?" (I never did find out if "Commodore" was his first name or if it was a title. The rumor floating around was that he was with the Treasury Department, not the EPA. This rumor was never confirmed.)

"Sure," Stan said. "I'd have thought you already would've seen them, though, as much flying over as you've done all week."

"Just keep calm, Mr. Rybachek," Mann said. "We only want to inspect your ponds."

"If you just wanted to inspect the ponds, why didn't you just drive here like the rest of the inspectors? Why did you have to try to scare us with your black helicopter and guns? You nearly killed one of our calves, and badly scared the horse. And why don't you know where the ponds are? You've been over them several times." Stan replied.

"We just want to inspect your ponds, Mr. Rybachek." Mann replied. "We're not looking for trouble." His actions belied his words.

We walked back towards the cabin with Mr. Mann; the other guy maintained his ten paces behind us.

As we neared the cabin, Cyndi came racing out, shouting, "Mom, Mom, I got the number!"

I replied, "Thanks, dear, but we did better than that, we got the helicopter. Its parked at the mine, and this is Mr. Mann. Dad and I are going to show him the settling ponds. You go back in the cabin and lock the door."

I didn't want to send Stan off alone with Mr. Mann, since the two "inspectors" were both armed. Mann did not have an assault rifle, but did carry a side arm, and it looked like a big one. I had the same feelings that our friend, Joe Vogler, had expressed to us. I probably would not see Stan again if I let him out of my sight, but I didn't think they would take both of us out, especially with Cyndi in the cabin.

We toured the settling ponds and Mr. Mann just nodded his head, and said, "Uh-huh." When we returned to the cabin, Stan and I told Mann that we would stay there for a while. We thought a cup of coffee might calm our nerves. Mr. Mann and his companion walked back to the mining operation, and soon we heard the roar of the helicopter as it sped off in the direction of Fairbanks. We felt like we'd dodged a bullet.

Cyndi and my sister Elizabeth spar over dishes in the cabin

Rose checks out her famous cranberry ketchup

CHAPTER 53

Stan and I concentrated on mining. We both had quit our jobs. He had been working for the Alaska Communication System, repairing teletype machines. He also served on the Alaska Water Board, appointed to the Board by Alaska Governor Cowper.

I had worked for KTVF, a local TV station. I started as a bookkeeper, but realized I could make more money selling advertising, so had switched to that. And, I was the hostess of a local TV talk show, called "Rose's Window." I had been able to take summers off, which was great for me.

We put together a Grand Plan as to how the mine would support us. Our plan included mining full time during the summer. But during the winter, Stan would make gold nugget jewelry and I would sell it, through home parties. We were the "Tupperware" of gold nugget jewelry. We printed catalogs in full color that we took to the parties.

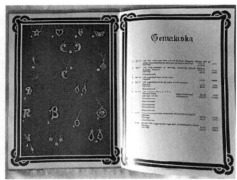

Our catalog, with gold jewelry pictured

The problems between the miners and the environmentalists and/or government continued to escalate. I was fortunate to be hired to write an opinion column for the Fairbanks Daily News Miner on Natural Resource Development. I must say, sometimes it was difficult to find something positive to write about. In addition to my column, I became the Editor of The Alaska Miner, a monthly publication of the Alaska Miners Association.

I was at home one morning when the phone rang. The pleasant voice on the other end introduced herself and said, "I am with Hour Magazine. We are doing a series for our show on Women in Alaska, and we wonder if you would agree to be on the show as our Mining Woman?"

"This is a pleasant surprise," I replied. "I would be more than happy to be on your show. When do you want to do it?" I hoped that it would offer some positive publicity for the mining industry.

We ironed out the details and on the allotted day, Stan, Cyndi and I met the film crew at our foot-bridge over the Tolovana river. The river was too high to drive across, so we had to walk across our suspension bridge. We had left the Weps on the mine-side of the river the last time we were at the mine. The film crew loaded their equipment into it, but opted to walk instead of riding. I guess they were afraid of my driving.

We spent some time at the cabin while I cooked Sourdough pancakes for them all, and we discussed the show. They were impressed with the moose steak, but most of them only took a tiny taste. Then we walked to the mine site, and they filmed while we washed the face. I did an interview with one of the crew, and we were on our way back to Fairbanks again.

This was a fifteen-minute segment which did not air in Fairbanks. However, they did send me a copy of the tape, so I got to watch it. Hour Magazine was hosted by Gary Collins. I was a little disappointed not to get to meet Gary, but when the segment aired, you would have thought it was he that was doing the interview. Sneaky, I thought!

Anyway, that segment on Women in Alaska aired several times during the 1980s. I would often get a comment from a friend or relative saying they'd seen me on TV.

Gary Collins, host of Hour Magazine, which aired on National Television from 1980 through 1989

CHAPTER 54

In 1986 we became grandparents, and I was also elected President of the Alaska Miners Association. The week of my election, EPA filed suit against five placer mining operations. Our operation on Wilbur Creek was one of those cited. They claimed alleged violations of the Clean Water Act and were asking for fines, ranging from a low of $30,000 to over $1,000,000.00. Our proposed fine was one of the larger ones.

The five of us contacted a highly-recommended attorney in Anchorage. We met with him, since we were all in Anchorage for the Convention. His recommendation? Settle!

Most of the miners decided to take his advice and settle. Stan and I talked it over and decided that we would rather fight than give up so easily. We decided we could act as *pro se* litigants and defend ourselves.

Having heard the adage that a good defense is a good offense, we challenged the 6000 pages of regulations that EPA had recently added to their Code of Federal Regulations (CFR's). We argued they had not listened to any of the public comments. And along with some of the other miners and miner's groups, we asked for an Evidentiary Hearing.

We also filed suit against some of the individual inspectors working out of Seattle's EPA region 10. We were busy with learning how to write briefs, and how to do research at the law library, plus still trying to make a living at the mine. We had lots of sleepless nights as we pondered what our next move should be. We even filed with the US Claims Court, claiming that EPA was "taking" our rights to mine our patented property. It was a busy time.

In July, we received a certified letter notifying us that EPA was planning to take our depositions in August. Of course, it was during our short sluicing season. We tried to get the depositions postponed but that request was denied, so we had to appear. They deposed me for three days. There were three attorneys asking questions, and they kept asking the same questions over and over. It got tiresome after a while, but I hid my exasperation.

We came home to North Pole after the end of my deposition on a Wednesday night and spotted a white thing stuck in our front door.

"What do you think that is?" I asked Stan as we drove into our driveway. We usually parked in the garage and entered the house through the back door. "If it wasn't so white, we might not have found it for days."

"I have no idea, but I'll go get it," he replied.

He came into the house with a business card in his hand. "Look at this," he said. "It's a card from an IRS agent. There's no writing on the card, or any indication as to what he might want with us. I have my doubts that this is really from the IRS, since I don't think they make house calls. Any ideas?"

"Well, if there's no note, I say we toss it." I replied. "I wouldn't put it past those EPA attorneys to put him up to this, if this even came from a real IRS agent, just to add more stress to their depositions. Or, it could just be a card that one of them had and stuck on our door. They just finished with me, but if I were you, I wouldn't mention this when they depose you."

Stan did not mention the card, and after his two solid days of depositions, we were finally free to get back to our sluicing. We never heard from the IRS agent. And we doubted that he even knew we had his card.

It was a relief to get back to the mine, and get busy sluicing again.

Sluicing

Loading the sluice box with the D-8

CHAPTER 55

Sluicing was going well, although we hated to leave Cyndi home alone for so long. She was a Junior in high school that fall. We had survived our depositions, we had our moose hanging, but we were about a week late in finishing our sluicing. We were afraid that it might turn cold, and freeze everything before we could finish.

We had just gotten into bed for the night, after a grueling day of sluicing, when we were startled to hear a vehicle drive into our yard. Getting dressed, we peered out the window and saw that it was Sallie. Not again!

"I have some more bad news for you," Sallie said. "When Cyndi got home from school today she found the house had been broken into. She's all right, and she's staying at my house, but we thought you ought to know. We called the cops, and they came and fixed the front door so it'll stay shut."

That ended our mining for the season. We went back to bed, and early the next morning started winterizing the operation. We drained the pumps, broke apart the pipeline, and cleaned up the sluice box. We loaded everything from the cabin that would freeze, and headed on down the road. Our sluicing would have to wait for another year. It was late afternoon before we could get back to town.

"What happened?" Stan asked Cyndi.

"Well, school got out for the day and my friend and I decided we'd go tanning. We've been so busy applying to all those colleges, that we both had headaches. I dropped her off at her house after we finished tanning and came on home.

"I noticed the light was on in the hall, and I thought you guys had forgotten to shut it off before you left, and I'd have to really get after you for leaving it on.

"Then, I noticed that the gun cabinet was trashed, and the guns were missing. Some of the living room chairs were turned over, and I was wondering what kind of party you had before you left. It wasn't until I went into my bedroom and saw the VCR sitting on my bed that I realized someone must have broken into the house.

"I called Sallie, and she was worried that they might still be in the house. She said she'd send Ron right over. Then I raced to the garage and grabbed the rake. I figured if they were still in the house, I needed something to defend myself with. I was never so scared in my life."

Upon investigating, we discovered that the burglar or burglars had concentrated on ransacking the garage, where Stan had his workshop. There had been some unfinished jewelry stored there. They had also done quite a bit of damage in the living room, and many items were missing from each area, including the prime furs I had kept from our trapping days. Our beloved wolverine was gone. Our guns were all gone, and lots of jewelry and jewelry making supplies were missing.

We were fortunate we had insurance and it mostly covered the loss. But some things could never be replaced, like the old 1890 Winchester 7.62 mm rifle my Dad had bought for me when I was in the eighth-grade. I had enjoyed some marvelous hunts with that rifle.

A couple of days later, we thought we probably should go back to the mine. It would be prudent to make sure we had everything winterized, since we'd left in such a hurry. Cyndi said that she was NOT afraid to stay home alone. Before we left, Stan gave her his .357 pistol.

That night at around 1:00 am, Cyndi was home watching TV, when she saw a car slowly driving down the highway. It backed up, and then went forward again, and stopped right near the end of our driveway.

Remembering that she had her Dad's .357, she stealthily made her way into her bedroom where she had it hidden. She watched as the people got out of the car, and milled about. She finally decided the gun would do her no good unless it was cocked, so she cocked it. She was relieved when the people all got back into their car, and drove away.

However, she was then faced with a dilemma. How to un-cock the gun? Her Dad had not showed her how to do that. She decided to call the North Pole Police non-emergency line.

The dispatcher answered and Cyndi said, in a calm voice, "So … can you please tell me how to un-cock a loaded gun?"

The dispatcher was a little shocked by the question, but asked for more information. Cyndi explained what had happened, and the dispatcher laughed, and said she would send a policeman over. Not to worry!

The policeman arrived, and soon the gun was safely residing once more under her mattress. Stan and I were quite appalled when we got home and learned about Cyndi's latest experience.

"You actually cocked the gun and then couldn't get it un-cocked?" I asked.

"Yes. Well, I thought about going outside and shooting it into the ground but I figured the neighbors might wonder about a shot being fired in the middle of the night. Since Suzie worked for the North Pole Police, I thought they might be able to help me. And they did."

"I think I'll install one of those phone burglar alarms," Stan said, shortly after that episode. "That way, if we are burglarized again, maybe we can catch them."

He checked out what would work and what wouldn't, and soon had a burglar alarm hiding in a closet. It had several sensors, so if any door was opened, and the code was not punched in, it would call up to three numbers.

We checked with the North Pole Police. They were not willing to have their number programmed into our alarm so we programmed in Sallie's number. We were hoping that it would never be needed.

Our house in North Pole

Barn at North Pole. At least, the burglars left the barn alone

CHAPTER 56

Winter had passed, and I held numerous gold-nugget jewelry parties and Stan was busy making jewelry. School was over for the year. One of Cyndi's teachers wanted her to stay at her house and take care of her dogs, while the teacher was on vacation. We were at the mine once again.

Sallie got a phone call from our alarm and could hear people moving around in our house. She immediately called the North Pole Police, and then she and Ron raced over to our house. When they arrived, there was a police car in the driveway.

"We didn't find anyone in the house," the policeman said. "We knocked on the door and no one answered. We couldn't go in, since you're outside the city limits, so we just waited."

Sallie unlocked the front door, and they all entered the house. They found a pile of things that had been removed from Cyndi's bedroom and was now stacked on the kitchen floor. They also found another stack of things piled in the bathroom and they found the back door standing wide open. They repaired the back door and reset the alarm.

Once again, we were awakened at the mine by the sound of a vehicle driving up. And, once again, it was Sallie.

"It happened again," she said. "You have been burglarized. I don't think they got away with much this time, because when the police drove up, it scared them, and they ran into the woods. But they had a pile of things in the kitchen and in the bathroom. You probably should come back home, and see if you can find anything missing. The North Pole Police also want to see you."

Back to North Pole we went the next morning. After trying to do an inventory, we went to visit with the North Pole Police. The captain said, "You do seem to be on someone's list. We have decided we'll let you program our number into your burglar alarm. Maybe that way, we'll be able to get there sooner in case of another burglary."

This was good news, and we took them up on it.

CHAPTR 57

We were thrilled when the State of Alaska recognized the contribution placer mining made to the economy of Alaska. They realized that the industry was in jeopardy and decided to do something positive.

They enacted legislation that established an Innovative Grants Program, and made available grants of $100,000 to individual miners that qualified. They geared the program for two different areas. One was to help miners develop technology for pollution control, and the second was to develop technology that would assist miners with gold recovery and water use reduction.

Stan said to me one morning, "I've been thinking, and I think we should apply for one or both of those grants."

"What kind of a project could we propose?" I asked. "We don't have room to build any better settling ponds than we already have. We've talked about pumping our wastewater out to the flat where we might have better treatment options, but I don't think that's very innovative. What are you thinking?"

"I think we should go underground," Stan said. "They have that perma-frost tunnel near Fairbanks, and I'll bet the perma-frost is warmer there than it is at the mine. We could either use steam to thaw, like the old timers did, or we could drill and blast. With the vertical face that we have now, we could put an adit (a mining term for an entrance) right into the face. We could use a truck to haul the gravel over to that area just above the duck pond. There, we could build a closed-circuit sluicing area, and not have any discharge at all.

"I think I'll go ask Dr. Skudrzyk at the University of Alaska if he'd be willing to help us with the details, since we'd have to have drawings and a lot of technical information to qualify for the grant. I've talked to Frank before, and he has always been friendly and willing to help."

He set up a meeting with Dr. Frank Skudrzyk, and Frank was more than willing to help. "It will get me out in the field," he said. "I love hands-on work."

Frank met with us at the mine, and we looked at various options. He thought that the drill and blast method should be the preferred method, since steam put a lot of heat into the workings, and we wanted them to stay frozen. He prepared the grant applications, and we waited to hear the results. We were thrilled when we were awarded both grants. Then the work began. Stan had to get the equipment ordered and we had to build a shed to house the equipment once it arrived.

"We'll sluice early this year," Stan said. "We need to be done early in August, so we'll have time to get the shed up. The equipment will be here in late September."

We ran the pump more often than usual, since it was a wet year with plenty of water. With the extra washing, the overhang grew and grew. By the time we could start sluicing, it was like a huge football field under the overhang. This massive overhang did not deter Stan from going under it with the dozer, so he could get all the thawed gravel sluiced.

I was quite fascinated by the overhang we had, and wondered what was keeping it up. The ice must have been very strong. I talked my mother into going underneath the overhang, so I could take her picture.

She looked like a speck under that massive overhang.

Mom under the ice overhang

Once the sluicing was finished, we moved the sluice box, the dragline, and the dozer out of the mining area. Stan sawed down several large trees, and flattened them on top before embedding them in the gravel, to use as a foundation for our shed. We had them in place, when it was time to make another trip to town.

Foundation

With our various lawsuits active, we needed to check the mail often in case some time-sensitive document arrived. Besides, Stan needed to get the lumber ordered for the shed.

There was a document that needed attention, so I opted to stay home and work on it, while Stan and the deliveryman hauled the lumber to the mine. I was just putting the finishing touches on our reply to the document that evening, when Stan returned.

He looked pale as a ghost, and his face was drawn.

"What happened?" I anxiously asked.

"You will never believe it," he replied. "You know that overhang you've been worried about all summer? Well, it fell. It looks like a field of huge ice cubes. Even the fuel tanks have been tossed about; it was a good thing they were empty. I don't know where all the ice and trees and stuff came from, but it's really a disaster. Our foundation is completely buried. I didn't know what to do with the lumber, but it looked like the east side of the mine hadn't been quite as damaged, so I had him unload it there. We'll have to see if I can make another level spot with the dozer before we can work on another foundation. We sure are lucky we moved the equipment, or it would all be buried under tons of ice!"

Cyndi and Stan stand on the wreckage

The next day Mom, Cyndi and I went with him to look at the disaster. And, a disaster it was. Chunks of ice bigger than some houses were laying helter-skelter everywhere. The ice seemed to have multiplied two-fold when it fell. Just a few days before, both Stan and Mom had been under that overhang. Talk about luck!

Our Red Truck parked by the boulders of ice

CHAPTER 58

Stan managed to get an area cleared and leveled so that we could build the shed. He sawed down more trees, and flattened the logs, and we replaced the foundation. Then it was time to put up the walls and roof. Stan sawed more trees, and we stood them upright, with a tree to use as a ridgepole on top. It was interesting trying to get those vertical logs in place without them falling on us, but we managed. We pulled our small travel trailer up from North Pole, and put it in one corner of our building. Then, we enclosed that area for a living space.

We only put a floor in the living space, leaving gravel as the floor for the rest of the building. We insulated the ceiling and walls of the entire shed, so it would stay warm during the winter, and we installed two oil-burning heaters.

Our fourteen-foot diameter culvert had been delivered … in pieces. We constructed it and fortunately moved it to a safe place before the collapse. The area where we had intended to insert the culvert was also under mounds of ice, but Stan came up with an alternative plan for installation.

Working on the culvert before the cave-in. Fortunately, we had moved the completed culvert before the cave in

New site for culvert

We were happy once our equipment arrived, and we got it parked in the completed building. The best news of all was that it fit like a glove. We even had room for the trailer carrying our water tank, plus the small dozer that we would use for hauling water. There was no wasted space when everything was in the building.

We needed a source of water for the winter, since the drill was water-cooled. Stan was convinced he could saw a hole in the ice of the river and get all the water he needed. It worked! After his beaver trapping, he had experience making holes in the river.

Our drill was a one-boom Jumbo, and one of our friends (Mike) was going to operate it. He planned to help Stan all winter, so he could gain experience mining in frozen ground. He had been a hard-rock miner in Montana before coming to Alaska.

Drill

We also had a load haul dump. It was a low-profile loader that could go either forwards or backwards, with the operator sitting in the middle, facing across the machine. It was quite an apparatus.

Load Haul Dump, or LHD

And, finally we had a 12/14-yard dump truck that would just fit nicely in the culvert. Our plan was to be able to turn it around in the workings, which we did.

Dump truck

Stan asked some friends to come help get the culvert installed for the adit, and the project went well.

Culvert on left, poised for its new home

The culvert was perfect as an entryway. Soon, Stan and Mike were ready to get started with mining.

Loading holes with explosives

I planned to stay in town with Cyndi during the winter and attend to our various legal battles. However, I would deliver frozen dinners to the guys periodically.

They had a large generator to operate the fans in the mine. This gave them plenty of electricity so they could microwave the dinners I brought. As they found out, the generator put off so much heat, they had to leave the large garage doors open when they were using it, no matter what the outside temperature was. At minus 30°F, they still had to open the doors. They didn't operate the machinery when it was colder than that.

The winter passed quickly. I was still busy with our legal battles, and cooking and delivering the meals. They were busily stockpiling gravel for sluicing in the spring. It was always fun to don a hard-hat and go into the mine to see their progress.

Dr. Skudrzyk made numerous visits to the mine. In the spring, a graduate student stayed with Stan and Mike for about six-weeks, while he wrote the thesis for his Master's degree. As the days grew longer and warmer, it would thaw during the day, but still freeze at night; they started only working the night shift. Soon, even that was too risky, so they brought in a load of hay bales, and filled the adit with them to insulate the workings for the summer.

They used plywood to seal the hay bales, and the adit was "summarized."

Adit sealed for the summer

Cyndi and I moved to the mine, once school was out and the adit was sealed. It was time for sluicing. It only took about six-weeks to sluice all the winter's stockpile. This was much easier mining than the old-fashioned way, although, it had taken us all winter to remove the gravel.

With winters being devoted to mining, our gold nugget jewelry parties faded. There was no time for Stan to make jewelry. He didn't want to spend his summers making jewelry. He had more important things to do, like go fishing.

Stan uses the small dozer to feed the gravels into the sluice box, while Rose supervises

CHAPTER 59

That fall, Cyndi headed off to college at New Mexico Tech in Socorro, NM. She was studying Mining Engineering. We decided to attend the Alaska Miners Association convention in Anchorage in November. We had an enjoyable time at the Convention. It was almost finished when we got a phone call from Sallie.

"We caught the burglars!" she excitedly proclaimed. "Your burglar alarm worked really well and called the North Pole Police, then called us. Apparently, there were two burglars, and they each had different cars. There was about six-inches of new snow, and their tracks led right up to the front door. When the alarm called the North Pole Police, the cops immediately drove over to the house. But since your house is outside the city limits, they thought they should probably wait for the State Troopers to show up. But then they saw one of the burglars run from behind the house and go west towards the road, while they saw the other one split and race the other direction. They tracked the one that went away from North Pole, and found where he had gotten into his parked car and driven away. Another North Pole cop was monitoring the radio and drove to the neighborhood. He saw a guy run out of the woods, and get into a car, so he wrote down the license plate number. They ran the plate, and then they went to his address. His car engine was still warm, and he was inside the apartment. I think he confessed to the burglary. I also think he gave them the name of his accomplice. One of them is named Manfred West, and I can't remember the other one."

When we returned from Anchorage, we found another bundle of things piled up to take; this time, they were from our bedroom and the radio room. We had been burglarized three times that year, and every time the burglars concentrated on a different part of the house. Was it the same burglars?

We asked the State Troopers if we could talk to Mr. West and ask him if he had burglarized our house before. We were told in no uncertain terms that if we even so much as mentioned the other burglaries, they would drop the case and turn him loose. We kept our mouths shut.

CHAPTER 60

The next winter Stan and I continued the underground mining operation. We planned to go into Fairbanks once a week or more often if need be, to check the mail. Mail delivery to Livengood had ended long before.

Since Mike had been operating the drill, and was no longer with us, it now fell on my shoulders to figure out how to run it. If I could run the dragline, this should be simple, right? There were only about a dozen levers that controlled the drill. It could be raised or lowered, shifted to one side or another, drill at any angle you might want, and all you had to do was move the right lever at the right time.

We moved from our cabin into the building with all the equipment, and were ready to get started. Removing the hay from the adit was easy, and we found that it had worked well as insulation, keeping the underground workings from thawing. We were ready.

It was exciting the first day as I drove the long-nosed drill, following Stan as he used the dozer to pull the water wagon into the adit. He hooked up the water to the drill, and proceeded to show me how to drill the blast holes.

My first experience trying to drill a hole was a complete disaster. I could not get it anywhere near where Stan wanted it. But soon I got the hang of it, and could almost drill where he indicated. Once a hole was drilled, Stan blew it out using an air compressor. He then put an electric cap into a stick of explosives. We used the Tovex brand since it was supposed to be much safer and easier to use than regular dynamite. He would run the lead of the cap out of the hole and tie it into the other leads. Then, when all the holes were ready, he would blow ammonium nitrate into the holes and seal them with a plug.

We then drove the drill and dozer out of the adit and parked them once more in the shed. It was always fun to watch as Stan connected the leads to the plunger, and then either he or I would push it down and wait for the explosions. We could count the different holes as they blew, since they were all timed to go in a special sequence. It was always a relief then we counted the ten holes we had drilled.

Next, it was time to get the fans going to blow the exhaust out of the work area so it would be safe to haul the ore. It didn't take long for those large fans to do their work, and the air was clear again. They also blew freezing air into the work area, so the permafrost remained frozen.

The next step was for Stan to take the dump truck underground, turn it around, and park it. He loaded it using the load-haul dump and hauled the ore to our stockpile. He could dump quite a few loads on the stockpile before he had to start the D-8 and flatten it out. Once he had it flat, he could start all over again with more loads. Our stockpile kept growing, and before spring, we had more gravel to sluice than they had the year before.

We continued, drilling, blasting, blowing and hauling. While Stan was busy hauling, I was busy writing briefs on an Osborne. It was a "portable" computer with a four-inch screen. It sure beat the old typewriter!

Osborne, first portable computer, manufactured in 1981

Loading holes

Exiting adit

CHAPTER 61

The grant required we mine at least four years. And, we were required to keep accurate records as we went along.

I thoroughly loved being at the mine in the winter again. Often, we would go outside, and enjoy the Northern Lights in all their glory. Usually they were white, but occasionally they were colored, with reds, greens, and even blues. Since the building was in a "cul-de-sac" with hills all around from the hydraulic mining days, except for a gap where the creek had been, it was like living in a fish bowl. The lights would dance across the entire visible sky. On a rare occasion, we could even hear them crackling. We would often just stand out there looking up, until we realized we were cold, and needed to warm up.

We could mine until the temperatures reached minus 30°F, and then it was time to just stay indoors and work on our legal briefs. We were lucky, though, that the temperature underground stayed at a pleasant twenty-nine degrees. We had thermometers in several places, to watch the temperatures. It might be cold getting to the adit, but was comfy once there.

Winter passed and soon it was time to close the adit for another summer. The bales of hay were getting a bit ragged, so we had to bring in a few extra ones. With the mine 'summarized," it was time to think about sluicing again. It was a simple project to put the pipeline back together and get the pump going.

Again, it was my job to run the dragline. It didn't have an electric starter, so Stan would have to crank it for me. However, once the tailings were stacked, I could shut it down, and watch as the water flowed through the riffles, washing the ore.

"Hey, come look at this!" Stan exclaimed one day. "Do you see that?"

Most of the gold we recovered was in the form of nuggets that were about a sixteenth of an inch in diameter. We had a few that were smaller, and sometimes, we would find a larger one. I walked over to see what had excited Stan, and there lying on top of the first riffle, was a large nugget. When we weighed it, it was nearly two-ounces! We hoped it had many brothers, but if it did, they remained hidden.

We sluiced for about seven weeks, and then all the gravel had been processed.

We still had not come to trial on the EPA lawsuit against us. But, a court date had been set for the fall of 1993. We decided that before our trial, we should travel to EPA Region 10 headquarters in Seattle, and depose several employees. This included Robbie Russel, the Region10 director. Bright and early one morning, we boarded the airplane for a flight to Seattle, with a huge box of documents.

We had scheduled times for doing the depositions of each one. After wandering around the headquarters for a while, trying to find the deposition room, we conducted our very first deposition. It was quite an experience. We ended up deposing ten employees of Region 10, and in every deposition, we asked about Commodore Mann. Would you believe that not one of the hierarchy of Region 10 would admit they knew anything about Mr. Mann?

However, it was quite interesting getting to ask other questions we felt pertinent, and getting what we thought was the "run-around" from everyone. We had to keep reminding the folks they were under oath. We thought Mr. Russel especially gave us the "run-around." He could not remember anything. Later, we talked to one of the EPA attorneys.

"You know," he said. "This is the first-time Robbie Russel has been deposed since he took over this office. He just isn't used to having to answer questions, especially from lay persons."

We had transcripts of the depositions with lots of information to review for the months before our court date.

CHAPTER 62

"Do you think we have time to attend the Miners Association Convention in Anchorage?" Stan asked me one morning. "They have some good speakers this year, and it would be fun to mingle with the few placer miners that are still mining. I heard there were less than a hundred left. EPA is making good on their promise to kill the industry. Besides, the larger hard-rock mines are getting active, and it would be fun to see what they're doing."

"That sounds like a great idea," I replied. "I'm almost finished going through the depositions, and Mom is in Anchorage with Henry and Debbie. I think she's about ready to come here for a visit, and she could ride back with us instead of flying."

We enjoyed the Convention, and were soon all three on our way back home. We were cruising along the highway as we neared Fairbanks, and felt lucky to have a green light at the very first intersection we came to as we entered town. There was a car stopped across the intersection in the left turn lane. However, as we were going through the intersection, it suddenly took off, and there was no way that Stan could avoid the head-on collision that followed. We later found out the driver was a sixteen-year old girl that had just passed her driver's test that day, after trying and failing three-times.

She was driving with her seventeen-year-old friend, and apparently talking up a storm. The friend suffered a broken back.

Mom was unconscious in the back seat and I feared she was dead. I thought Stan and I were unscathed, but talking to people afterwards, I realized we had both been unconscious for about ten minutes. Stan was very worried because our dog was missing. My door had popped open, and the dog had jumped out and disappeared. It was utter chaos for a while.

Fortunately, someone had a car phone and called 911, and the ambulance showed up to take Mom to the hospital. Another ambulance soon came, and they decided I needed hospital care, too. They wanted to take Stan to the hospital, too, but he was worried about the dog. It was a while before a bystander found the dog and delivered him to Stan. Stan would not leave him until he was sure someone was going to take care of him.

Even though my seat belt was fastened, I hit my head on the windshield hard enough to crack it (the windshield, not my head). I had a couple of broken ribs, from the seat belt that had no doubt saved my life. I was hospitalized for a few days.

Stan was checked over and released. He had bruises and some long-lasting injuries. Our dog was fine.

Mom had more serious injuries and ended up having surgery. Her whole face was swollen and black and blue, and she looked awful. After she was released from the hospital, she went back to Anchorage with my sister and brother.

I was diagnosed with a closed-head injury, and I had a lot of trouble trying to cope with simple chores, like taking a shower. Our court date was looming, so we asked for a continuance, which was granted. However, it was only for ninety-days. And, I did not improve that quickly. I was befuddled, confused, and just unable to function. We asked for a further continuance but our request was denied.

We tried to hire an attorney but couldn't find one to take our case.

Stan met with the EPA attorneys, and settled our case. Not only that case, but settled all the other cases that were still pending. They required that we drop them all if we wanted to settle the one they had filed against us. We were finished being pro se litigants.

We still had one year left to comply with the grant requirements, so we tried to go back to our underground mining.

We could hardly function, but we managed to get enough ore removed to satisfy the grant requirements. It was with sadness that we parked the equipment for the summer and sluiced that last bit of gravel.

We hoped we would be well enough to get back to mining in a year or so. Hope springs eternal, according to Alexander Pope.

* * *

During the summer of 1993, Manfred West, who had been convicted of burglarizing our house in North Pole, walked away from a half-way house near Fairbanks. We were concerned that he might come looking for us, but we never saw him. However, soon after Mr. West was on the loose, our friend Joe Vogler disappeared. A neighbor had gone by his place, and found his dogs and pet goose starving. Joe was nowhere to be found. This set off a massive man hunt. Posters were everywhere, "Where is Joe Vogler?"

Joe, at the age of 80, was a very colorful character. He was a three-time gubernatorial candidate in Alaska and founder of the Alaska Independence Party (AIP). The AIP had been successful in electing a governor, Governor Walter J. Hickel. Governor Hickel had been elected as governor of Alaska in 1966, but had resigned to assume the position of Secretary of the Interior. He was reelected in 1990.

Joe was also an advocate for abolishing statehood and becoming an independent nation. He was convinced that the options open for voters when Alaska and Hawaii entered the Union did not conform with the United Nation's charter. In fact, he was scheduled to appear before the United Nations to address that issue just a few weeks after his disappearance, in May 1993.

Joe's body was not found until October 1994, but the authorities did find Manfred West, and he confessed to killing Joe. They eventually found Joe based on information provided by Manfred West. One of the rumors around was that West was a contract hitter, that he worked for felonious folks, and did other odd jobs for various crime-related syndicates.

We thought how lucky we were to be in Anchorage at the time of our burglary. If the earlier burglaries were related as we suspected, we were glad Cyndi didn't corner the burglar armed with the garden rake, and that in the three burglaries we suffered nothing more terrible happened than missing property. Although Joe was an eccentric and controversial character, we were saddened by what happened to him.

But questions remained. Questions like were the crimes against us and Joe related? Were we lucky to be alive? Those questions will no doubt never be answered. But, Manfred West's eighty-year sentence for Joe's murder closes that chapter of our lives.

CHAPTER 63

We were never able to mine after our motor-vehicle accident, but we did spend many joyful hours at the mine, fishing for grayling from the bridge, picking berries in the summer, and hunting moose during the fall and winter. We often made trips to the mine on our snow machine, and would spend a few days reminiscing and enjoying being once again in a place that had provided us with so much pleasure.

Both Suzie and Sallie married and had families. Cyndi got her Bachelors and Master's degrees in Mining Engineering, and then decided to go to law school. She stayed in New Mexico, married there, and has a family. All the kids enjoyed joining us at the mine whenever they could get away.

Jennifer, Sallie's daughter, had a severe allergy to cats. She would get sick every time she visited at our house in North Pole. Since we had my cat Herkimer at our house in North Pole, we moved him to the mine, hoping that would purify our house. It didn't work!

One summer our friends from Texas, Joe and Annie, came visiting. They drove their fifth-wheel across the river and parked in the yard. Sallie and daughter Jennifer came to spend the weekend. Jennifer immediately started choking up upon entering the cabin, so Sallie erected a two-man tent in the yard. She and Jennifer stayed the night in the tent.

Annie knocked on our door bright and early the next morning. "I just wanted to tell you that you had a bear roaming around last night," she said in a solemn voice. "I just happened to look out the window and saw it going around a corner of the house. I just watched, and soon it came back around, and came right up to our fifth-wheel. I watched as it circled around, and every so often, it would stand on its hind legs and try to peek in a window. I finally yelled at it, and it dropped down on all fours and ran down the road."

"I wonder how Sallie fared," I asked. "Did you check on her?"

"No, but that tent is right around the corner where I saw that bear going."

Annie and I went out to check on the tent. We could see a long tear down the front of the canvas, which had no doubt been made by a bear's claw. It hadn't penetrated the inside liner, and the girls were still sleeping in the tent.

"Look up on the roof," Annie whispered, and there were muddy bear tracks wandering all over the roof.

"It looks like he climbed up that ladder," I said, "then he just wandered around up there. Why didn't the dogs alert us?"

When Sallie came in the cabin, looking well rested, we told her what we'd found. She had to race out and look at the tent, and there was that long slit. "I don't think I'll sleep in a tent here again," she said. And, she never did.

Muddy bear tracks on roof

257

Mom, Suzie with her two children, Jason and Stephanie and Sallie with her two children Jennifer and Brian enjoy being at the mine

CHAPTER 64

Mom was visiting us from Montana a few weeks later. Suzie, her husband Jerry, and their two kids (Jason and Stephanie) came from Seward. It would be the 4th of July in a couple of days. Sallie, Ron and their two kids (Jennifer and Brian) were expected to come, bearing fireworks. It was a bit dry, but we thought the fireworks would be safe.

"I think I'll teach all the kids how to pan for gold," Stan said. "After all, this was a gold mine, and they ought to know how to pan. So, after Sallie and Ron get here, I'll take the kids to the creek, and we'll have some lessons. You guys can cook lunch, and then we can do the fireworks."

Stan leads the procession of grands to pan

The kids were very excited about their lesson and were soon standing in the creek, intently watching as grandpa picked up a gold pan and showed them how to use it. He had enough gold pans for each of the kids to have one. The creek was quite low, due to the lack of rain, so no danger of the gold pans washing away.

They were all doing very well with their lesson, when Jason decided he needed a drink of water. He dropped his gold pan on the bank and went to the cabin. It wasn't long before he came racing back toward the creek, yelling at the top of his voice. "Come quick! Grandma is about to take her teeth out!"

Gold pans flew in all directions and all four of the kids stampeded towards the cabin, leaving Stan behind with a bewildered look on his face. He had to scurry around to collect the discarded gold pans. He never got over the fact that his gold panning was bested by his mother-in-law removing her false teeth.

We enjoyed our lunch, the steaks were barbequed to perfection, and the rest of the food was delicious. Then it was time to gather around for the fireworks. It was still daylight, but we thought we could probably see some of the bottle rockets, anyway. Stan found a nice metal tube, attached to a metal base, that he had used to hold welding rods. It would be perfect for the bottle rockets.

I hoped our Yorkie pup would enjoy the fireworks. We now had a full Yorkie, Mr. Buddy.

We had not had him long, and didn't know if he was afraid of loud noises or not, so I decided I would hold him while Jason and Stephanie set off the fireworks. We gathered around on some folding chairs and were all set for a delightful firework display.

When Stephanie lit the first bottle rocket, the fuse started sizzling, and Mr. Buddy tried to jump off my lap. I managed to hold him, but when the next one started sizzling, he got loose. Instead of heading for the house like I thought he would, he attacked the bottle rocket. He sent the whole thing flying, and about that time, it fired. It was twirling in the dirt and shooting little firework things every which direction.

One hit Sallie on the leg, and caused a large burn. Several landed in dried leaves, and started small fires. Fortunately, Ron tossed a bucket over the shooting rocket, so it quit firing flaming missiles. We had our work cut out for us trying to keep all the fires from spreading. We were happy when they were all out. We decided that perhaps we should stop the fireworks exhibition. A nice cool drink was in order.

Sallie put salve on her burn and declared herself well. And, we saved the remaining fireworks for the following year.

Anxiously awaiting the start of the fireworks

CHAPTER 65

Since we were not spending very much time at the mine, the squirrels moved in, and they were very destructive. When we did stay there, Stan started hunting them with his .22 rifle. Mr. Buddy began following Stan and once Stan had shot a squirrel, he nabbed it and raced off into the woods with it. This became great sport for him, and he loved it when anyone picked up the .22.

"Any idea where he's taking those squirrels?" I asked Stan one morning. "I think you've shot three of them this morning, and he's gotten them all."

"No," Stan replied. "I even tried following him, but I was making my way through the brush when he showed up behind me, without his squirrel."

One day, Mr. Buddy disappeared for a long time. We thought that a wolf or lynx had probably gotten him for dinner. We were mourning him when he showed up, quite bedraggled, but all in one piece. The next day he did his disappearing act again, and again we were worried. What could he be up to?

Finally, one-day Stan came in the house and said, "Guess what! I just happened to see Mr. Buddy sitting under a tree, looking up, and there in the tree was a squirrel. I think when he's been missing all those times, he has a squirrel treed and is waiting for one of us to come shoot it."

Stan grabbed his gun and went out to dispatch the squirrel. And soon Mr. Buddy was back in the house, without a squirrel, but happy as could be. He had grown tired of waiting for Stan to go squirrel hunting, and was trying it on his own. His only failure was not clueing us into what he was doing.

After that, when we noticed that Mr. Buddy was gone, either Stan or I would take the .22 single shot and see if we could find him. Most times we would find him sitting under a tree, and sure enough, there would be a squirrel up the tree. Often, they would be chattering, which made it easy to locate where he was, but sometimes they were quiet. This made it much more difficult to find Mr. Buddy. He was a dedicated hunter and would even disappear when it was raining. In those instances, we would put on our rain gear and go looking for him. Sometimes we would find him and sometimes we wouldn't. He often came in drenched from hunting in the rain.

Sue and Jerry and their family came for a visit. Stephanie and I went out looking for Mr. Buddy after he had been gone for quite some time. We found him, and I shot the squirrel. As he always did, Mr. Buddy grabbed the squirrel and disappeared in the willows. Instead of following me back to the cabin, Stephanie took off hot on his trail. They hadn't gone far, when Mr. Buddy, hearing someone following, dropped the squirrel. Stephanie picked it up and proudly brought it back to the house.

"Grandma, I found his squirrel. He just dropped it," she said. And, following behind her came a very dejected Mr. Buddy. She tried to give the squirrel back to him, but he would have nothing to do with it. He couldn't even eat his dinner that night, he was in such a funk. It took him two days to recover, and during all that time, he never went hunting squirrels again.

It wasn't until after Sue, Jerry and the kids left that he once again began disappearing. We were back to normal.

However, this time there was a slight change. Occasionally, he would bark. In that way we could find him, and dispatch the squirrel without hunting all over the countryside for him.

Cyndi traveled to Alaska with her husband Shawn in 2003. Shawn is adept at hunting and looked forward to seeing game in Alaska. When they visited the mining claims, Buddy had treed a squirrel, and their boy, Lane, was happy to shoot it for him. Shawn claimed the only animals he is sure are in Alaska are squirrels and one porcupine he happened to see from the highway.

We never did find Mr. Buddy's squirrel graveyard, but after that experience with Stephanie, we just gave up even looking for it.

CHAPTER 66

We were in Texas for the winter, when the phone rang.

"Hello," I cheerfully answered.

It was Sallie. "I'm afraid I have bad news again," she said. "Ron went up to the cabin today, and found that a bear had broken into it. He didn't have his gun, and he didn't know if the bear was still inside or not, but several of the windows were broken, and he could smell the bear."

"Oh, good grief," I said. "That's not good news. Well, we'll be home in a couple weeks, and I guess we can clean it up when we get there."

"We're going back up there tomorrow, and I'll take some pictures. Ron will have his gun, just in case the bear is still in the cabin. Most of the snow is gone, so he must have just roused from hibernating. Guess he was hungry." Sallie said.

The next day we received her pictures via e-mail. What a mess that bear had made. Flour was scattered far and wide. There appeared to be broken glass scattered around, the furniture was upset, and there was mud everywhere.

Needless to say, our trip back to Fairbanks was not a happy one, knowing we had a mess awaiting us. Once home, we soon gathered up some cleaning supplies, and went to the cabin.

When we walked into the bedroom, we noticed that the window over the bed had been broken, and you could see a trail of mud leading into the kitchen. The odor was overpowering. He was one stinky bear. The bedroom had not been badly ransacked, but the kitchen was a disaster area. We had left many staples in wall lockers, such as sugar and flour, and the bear had managed to open every door to the wall lockers. He had strewn flour everywhere, and broken the molasses jar, stirring that into the flour.

Doesn't that look appetizing?

He had broken a window over the sink, and another one over the wood box. And, it appeared that, like the three bears in Goldilocks, he had taken a nap on the bed. The bedspread was covered in mud. He must have been one muddy bear by the time he'd gotten into the cabin.

It didn't get any better

"Where do we start with this mess?" I asked Stan. "I have never seen such a disaster."

"Well, I think we'll get the scoop shovel and the regular shovel," he said.

"You can hold the scoop, and I'll shovel into it. Then we can dump it into a plastic garbage bag, and load it in the truck. We need to measure the broken windows, too. I don't think we can stay here tonight, but we can clean until we get tired, then go back to town. When we come up tomorrow, we can bring the glass. He *would* have to break three of our four windows. You'd think he could have come and gone through just one!"

We scooped and shoveled, and got the floor clean enough to sweep and mop. Then it was time to head for Fairbanks, with our fifteen-bags of trash. Where did all that stuff come from?

We found the empty flour sack in the mess, but the 50-pound sugar bag, and the 25-pound brown sugar bags had disappeared. Stan found them both a few days later about half a mile from the cabin. How that bear managed to crawl out the windows carrying the nearly full bags was baffling, but he apparently did.

The next day, we continued cleaning. I could salvage some things that had been in the cupboards, like spices. While he had swatted them all down into his mess, they were uninjured. He had also emptied the cupboard of plates, glasses, and cups. A few of them were unbroken, but most were smashed. This was what had created the broken glass that we'd scooped up and hauled away in the garbage bags. Fortunately, he had not been able to open the one cupboard that contained my pots and pans, so they were unscathed.

It took us several trips to get the place livable again. Stan made several forays into the woods, hunting the bear, but was never successful in finding him (or her). From the size of the print, and the outline of where it had stretched out on the bed, we figured it was no doubt an old bear that was toothless, and looking for an easy meal.

Bear Track – notice penny in center

However, we were not above hoping that the glass the bear had no doubt eaten would do some severe damage, and it would never return. It never did.

Stan repairs insulation knocked down by bear

Ketchup anyone?

CHAPTER 67

And, now it is time to write the final chapter in our lives as miners. Stan and I were spending the winter in South Texas, enjoying the warm weather, and visiting with our friends. We still had not recovered enough from our automobile injuries to return to mining.

It was Mother's Day when our phone rang, and it was Sallie. Poor Sallie, she was always the bearer of bad news. This time she was nearly in tears.

"I hate to tell you this," she said. "But, the cabin burned at the mine. One of my friends called and told me he'd been driving down the Elliott Highway and had seen a pickup off a drop-off by the access road, and the pickup had been burned. Ron and I went up, and we found the pickup.

Then, the cable across the road had been knocked down. The river went out the week before, so it was high water with floating ice chunks. We had to park in the gravel pit and walk across the bridge. We found the four-wheeler at the bottom of the hill just before you get to the cabin. It had apparently stalled, and the thieves couldn't get it running again, so they'd just left it. And, the cabin was completely gone. Burned to the ground. Only some twisted remnants of beds, and the refrigerator remain."

"Did you call the Troopers?" Stan asked.

"Yes, they went up to investigate. I'll let you know what they find," she said.

Sallie called again that night. "Well, the Trooper said it appeared the arsonists had stayed around the place watching it burn, and when sparks landed in some of the trees nearby, they had put out the fires. He said if they hadn't done that, probably everything else would have gone up in flames, too. He said they would talk to the person whose truck was wrecked and burned near the Elliott Highway. If I hear anything more, I'll let you know."

She called us a few days later, and said. "The Trooper just called back, and said he'd talked to the owner of that pickup. The owner told the Trooper that he and a friend had taken his pickup and gone fishing at the Tolovana bridge, just a few miles from the mine site. While they were fishing, someone had stolen his truck, and he hadn't seen it since. The Trooper said he found that story hard to believe, but both guys swore that's what happened."

When we got back to Fairbanks a few weeks later, we reluctantly drove to the mine. The burned pickup was sitting in the ditch near our access road. Very visible was the imprint of the cable in the radiator of the pickup. That pickup had definitely been used to break the cable loose. And, in the back of the pickup were several burned articles from our garage.

We always believed that the two "fishermen" had used the pickup to tear down the cable and driven up to the gravel pit. They had broken into the cabin and robbed it of anything they could carry, and then set fire to the cabin to hide evidence of their crime. They had the bad luck to slip off the access road trying to get back on the highway and got stuck as they were leaving. Not being able to get un-stuck, and with a load of stolen property in the pickup, they torched it, as they had the cabin. Their story that they were fishing was hard to believe. During breakup, no one in their right mind would even consider trying to fish!

Still, we could not prove that theory; it remains another unsolved mystery.

While it was never the same to visit the mine without our beloved cabin, we always remember the good times and treasure our experiences. And, we have golden memories of our cabin. While we never did strike it rich, we led a very rich and rewarding life Mining for Alaskan Adventures.

Mom in the kitchen at the mine. She was always cooking

Stan enjoys his coffee in cabin

First attempts at hydraulic mining

Sluicing the ore from underground mining. Rose operates dragline, while Stan supervises.

Made in the USA
Columbia, SC
28 October 2017